MEDITERRANEAN DIET FOR BEGINNERS
- 2023 Edition -

Easy and Delicious Recipes to Build a Healthy Lifestyle and Lose Weight. Discover the Secrets of Longevity and Well-Being With the Mediterranean Way Of Eating

All rights reserved. Copyright 2023.

Except as authorized by U.S. copyright law, no part of this book may be duplicated in any way without prior consent from the publisher or author.

Under no circumstances will the publisher or author bear any blame or legal liability for any harm, compensation, or financial loss caused by the material in this book.

With relation to the subject matter discussed, this book is intended to offer reliable information. It is offered for sale with the understanding that neither the author nor the publisher is engaged in providing accounting, legal, or other professional services.

Notwithstanding the publisher's and author's best efforts in the preparation of this book, they expressly disclaim any implied warranties of merchantability or suitability for a particular purpose and make no claims or guarantees regarding the accuracy or completeness of its information. Sales agents and written sales materials are not authorized to issue or extend any warranties. The suggestions and tactics offered here might not be appropriate for your circumstance. When necessary, you should seek expert advice. Any loss of profit or other financial losses, including but not limited to special, incidental, consequential, personal, or other consequences, is not the responsibility of the publisher or the author.

Table Of Contents

Introduction 7
   What is the Mediterranean diet? 7
   The benefits of the Mediterranean diet 7
   An interesting comparison with the other diets: Keto, Dash and Intermittent Fasting 8
   Your new shopping list and foods to avoid 11
   Olive oil: its properties and conservation techniques 13
   Questions beginners ask most often and answers 14

Recipes 15
   Breakfast recipes 15
      Greek yogurt scrambled eggs 15
      Bowl with millet and strawberries 15
      Bruschetta with Greek yogurt and tomatoes 16
      Dandelion bruschetta and yogurt 16
      Grain bowl with egg and avocado 17
      Semifreddo with blueberries and dried fruit 17
      Toast with egg and avocado with oriental flavours 18
      Tender frittata with herbs 18
      Avocado Cheese Omelette 19
      Nectarine peach bruschetta 19
      Bruschetta with spinach, squash and egg 20
      Nutritious spinach crepes 20
      Bruschetta with feta cheese and watermelon radishes 21
      Nutritious bowl with blueberries, dried fruits and granola 21
      Bowl of oats with banana and chocolate 22

   Pasta and Rice Entrées 22
      Pasta with tomato and basil 22
      Traditional Chicken Parmesan pasta 23
      Greek pasta with feta 23
      Vegetarian fettuccine with mushrooms 24
      Pesto pasta with asparagus and chicken 24
      Vegetarian ravioli with artichokes 25
      Tomato macaroni with fresh ricotta 25
      Delicious pasta with cherry tomatoes 26
      Summer pasta salad 26
      Pesto pasta with vegetables 27

- Greek rice with black beans ... 27
- Greek rice with lemon ... 28
- Mediterranean brown rice ... 28
- Fried rice with feta ... 29
- Traditional tomato rice ... 29
- Basmati rice with herbs ... 30
- Mediterranean rice with chicken powder ... 30
- Yummy rice with shrimps ... 31
- Traditional Italian rice salad ... 31
- Rice salad with salmon ... 32

Seafood, meat and poultry entrées ... 32
- Delicious cod with lemon ... 32
- Nutritious halibut with veggies ... 33
- Gourmet chicken with veggies ... 33
- Tasty sausages with peppers ... 34
- Chicken with tomatoes ... 35
- Greek style grouper ... 35
- Baked fish with tomatoes and spices ... 36
- Mediterranean Chicken Soup ... 36
- Greek chicken wings ... 37
- Chicken thighs with yogurt sauce ... 37
- Lemon flavoured salmon ... 38
- Salmon with balsamic glaze ... 38
- Salmon with feta and veggies ... 39
- Beef ribs in wine with potatoes ... 39
- Beef stew with green beans ... 40
- Italian fish soup ... 41
- Greek fish fillet ... 41
- Super tasty shrimps with bell peppers ... 42
- Middle Eastern lamb meatballs with onions ... 43
- Spanish-style chicken ... 43

Salad dishes ... 44
- Fresh fruit salad ... 44
- Greek-style tuna salad ... 45
- Mediterranean veggies salad ... 46
- Salad with watermelon and feta ... 46

- Tomato salad with feta 47
- Orange and pomegranate salad 47
- Berry salad with burrata and arugula 48
- Nutritious salad with avocado 48
- Salad with brussels sprouts and dried fruit 49
- Mediterranean panzanella salad 49
- Mix of brussels sprouts and mushrooms 50
- Asparagus salad with tomatoes 50
- Super tasty cherry tomatoes salad 51
- Tomato salad with burrata and prosciutto 51
- Gourmet Greek Chicken Salad 52

Appetizers 53
- Potato pancakes 53
- Middle eastern cheese rolls 53
- Pizza eggplant with mushrooms 54
- Feta croquettes with sesame and honey 55
- Grilled Margherita Pizza 55
- Delicious Greek pita with cheese and spinach 56
- Spanish bruschetta with tomato 56
- Yummy cauliflower fritters with mint yogurt 57
- Aperitif with salmon and mix of vegetables 57
- Bruschetta with feta and salmon 58
- Stuffed zucchini slices with feta and tomato 58
- Greek fried eggplant sticks 59
- Mini bruschetta with figs and goat cheese 59
- Sticks of meat with feta cheese 60
- Tasty Greek skewers 60

Desserts 61
- Special olive oil chocolate cake 61
- Traditional cannoli 62
- Mediterranean lemon cheesecake 63
- Homemade yogurt 63
- Tahini banana milkshake 64
- Fig dessert 64
- Carrot cake with honey 65
- Orange cake with pistachios 65

- French toast with honey and orange 66
- Olive oil orange cake 67
- Middle Eastern style ice cream with pistachios 67
- Sweet pumpkin parfait 68
- Greek yogurt with dried fruit 68
- Traditional apple strudel 69
- Mini bruschetta with Greek yogurt and peaches 69

28-Day Meal Plan 70

Conclusion 74

Introduction

What is the Mediterranean diet?

The Mediterranean diet is a way of eating that is rooted in the unique gastronomy of Greece, Italy, and other Mediterranean Sea countries.

The diet is developed on plant-based foods such whole grains, veggies, legumes, fruits, seeds, herbs, and nuts. The main source of fat is olive oil.

Fish, seafood, dairy, and chicken in moderation are permitted. Red meat and pastries are only eaten on special occasions. It is considered a way of life rather than the classic diet because it is not a rigid list of rules or restrictions, but rather a flexible and customizable approach to food.

The Mediterranean diet is a way of eating because it emphasizes whole, unprocessed foods and encourages a wide range of nutrient-dense foods such as fruits, vegetables, whole grains, legumes, and nuts. It also promotes the use of healthy fats, such as olive oil, and the consumption of fish and seafood as the primary sources of protein.

Unlike many traditional diets that are often restrictive and difficult to sustain over the long term, the Mediterranean diet is a more balanced and enjoyable way of eating that can be easily incorporated into daily life. It is a way of eating that is based on a healthy, balanced, and enjoyable approach to food and nutrition, rather than on strict rules and deprivation. the Mediterranean diet is often enjoyed as a social activity with family and friends in Mediterranean countries. Meals are typically eaten together, often with several courses and a variety of dishes made with fresh, locally sourced ingredients.

In Mediterranean cultures, meals are seen as a time for family and friends to gather and socialize, and food is often prepared with care and attention to detail. The focus is on enjoying the flavors and textures of fresh, seasonal ingredients, rather than on restrictive portion sizes or calorie counting.

Research has shown that the social aspect of the Mediterranean diet may contribute to its health benefits, as it promotes a relaxed and enjoyable approach to food and eating that can help to reduce stress and improve overall well-being.

So, in addition to its health benefits, the Mediterranean diet can also be a way to foster social connections and enjoy the company of loved ones around the table.

The benefits of the Mediterranean diet

The Mediterranean diet has numerous health benefits, including:

- Reduced risk of heart problems: The Mediterranean diet is rich in healthy fats, such as olive oil, and emphasizes whole, unprocessed foods, which may help to reduce the risk of heart disease. The Mediterranean diet has been shown to reduce the risk of heart disease because it emphasizes whole, nutrient-dense foods that are naturally low in saturated and trans fats, and high in healthy fats, fiber, and antioxidants. Here are some specific reasons why the Mediterranean diet may reduce the risk of heart disease:
- Reduces inflammation: The Mediterranean diet is rich in anti-inflammatory foods, such as fruits, vegetables, whole grains, and fatty fish. While chronic inflammation is a precursor to coronary artery disease, decreasing inflammation can aid in heart health.
- Improves cholesterol levels: The Mediterranean diet is high in monounsaturated and polyunsaturated fats. We can found them in olive oil, nuts, and fatty fish. These healthy fats can help to improve cholesterol levels by increasing the level of HDL cholesterol (the "good" cholesterol) and reducing the level of LDL cholesterol (the "bad" cholesterol).

- Lowers blood pressure: The Mediterranean diet is rich in potassium, which can help to decrease blood pressure. Additionally, the diet emphasizes whole, unprocessed foods that are naturally low in sodium, which can also contribute to lower blood pressure.
- Reduces oxidative stress: The Mediterranean diet is rich in antioxidants, such as vitamin C and E, which can help to reduce oxidative stress and improve heart health.
- Improves blood sugar control: The Mediterranean diet is heavy in fiber-rich foods including fruits, vegetables, and whole grains, which can aid with blood sugar regulation and lower the possibility of developing type 2 diabetes. Diabetes is a risk factor for heart issues, so improving blood sugar control can help to reduce the risk of heart disease as well.
- Lower risk of certain cancers: Studies have suggested that the Mediterranean diet may help to reduce the risk of certain types of cancer, such as breast and colorectal cancer.
- Improved brain function: The diet is rich in nutrients that are the basics for our brain health, such as omega-3 fatty acids and antioxidants, which help to strengthen our cognitive function and reduce the risk of dementia.
- Better weight management: The Mediterranean diet emphasizes whole, nutrient-dense foods and healthy fats, which may help to promote feelings of fullness and reduce the risk of overeating, leading to better weight management.
- Reduced inflammation: The diet is high in anti-inflammatory foods, such as fruits, vegetables, and fatty fish, which may help to reduce chronic inflammation and improve overall health.

Among other things, the Mediterranean diet can be helpful for weight loss because it emphasizes whole, nutrient-dense foods that are low in processed carbohydrates and added sugars, and high in fiber, protein, and healthy fats. Here are some reasons why the Mediterranean diet may be helpful for weight loss:

- Promotes satiety: The Mediterranean diet emphasizes whole, unprocessed foods that are high in fiber and protein, which can help to assure feelings of fullness and reduce the risk of overeating.
- Reduces cravings: The Mediterranean diet is low in processed carbohydrates and added sugars, which can help to reduce cravings for unhealthy, high-calorie foods.
- Encourages healthy fats: The Mediterranean diet emphasizes healthy fats, such as those found in olive oil, nuts, and fatty fish, which can help to promote feelings of satiety and reduce the risk of eating too much.
- Promotes balanced eating: The Mediterranean diet is a balanced and sustainable way of eating that encourages a variety of nutrient-dense foods, rather than restrictive diets that can be difficult to sustain over the long term.
- Supports a healthy lifestyle: The Mediterranean diet is not just about what you eat, but also about how you live. It encourages regular physical activity, stress reduction, and social connections, all of which can support a healthy weight and lifestyle.

An interesting comparison with the other diets: Keto, Dash and Intermittent Fasting

Let's start by comparing the Mediterranean diet to the keto diet. The Mediterranean diet is moderate in carbohydrates, with a focus on complex carbohydrates from whole, unprocessed foods. It also contains sufficient quantities of lean protein, such as poultry and fish, as well as a little quantity of red meat. The keto diet, on the other hand, is a very low-carbohydrate, high-fat diet that is intended to induce ketosis, a condition in which the body burns fat for fuel rather than carbs.

The keto diet typically includes high amounts of fat from sources such as butter, coconut oil, and fatty meats, as well as moderate amounts of protein and very low amounts of carbohydrates from non-starchy vegetables and small amounts of berries. While the Mediterranean diet includes healthy fats from sources such as olive oil and fatty fish, the keto diet emphasizes high amounts of fat, including saturated fat, from sources such as butter, coconut oil, and fatty meats.

Protein intake: The Mediterranean diet includes moderate amounts of lean protein, such as poultry and fish, while the keto diet includes moderate amounts of protein from sources such as meat, fish, and dairy products.

Sustainability: The Mediterranean diet is a balanced and sustainable way of eating that can be followed long-term, while the keto diet is often difficult to sustain over the long-term due to its restrictive nature.

But is it possible to follow these two diets at the same time?

The Mediterranean diet and the keto diet are quite different in terms of their macronutrient ratios and food choices, so it would be difficult to follow both diets simultaneously. The Mediterranean diet is moderate in carbohydrates, with a focus on whole, unprocessed foods that are high in fiber and nutrients, while the keto diet is very low in carbohydrates and high in fat.

Following both diets at the same time would be hard, as the macronutrient ratios are quite different. It could also be difficult to meet the nutrient needs of both diets simultaneously. For example, the Mediterranean diet emphasizes whole grains, fruits, and vegetables, which are important sources of fiber, vitamins, and minerals, while the keto diet restricts these foods in order to maintain a state of ketosis.

Additionally, it's worth noting that both diets have been associated with health benefits when followed properly, but they have different goals and purposes. The Mediterranean diet emphasizes whole, nutrient-dense foods, while the keto diet is often used for short-term weight loss or medical purposes under medical supervision.

Therefore, it is generally not recommended to try to follow both diets simultaneously.

Then let's move on to the analysis and comparison with the dash diet.

The DASH diet:

- Emphasizes fruits, vegetables, whole grains, lean protein, and low-fat dairy
- Low in saturated and trans fats, cholesterol, and added sugars
- Encourages the use of herbs and spices for flavor instead of salt
- Includes moderate amounts of nuts, seeds, and legumes
- Designed to lower blood pressure and reduce risk of heart disease
- Has also been associated with weight loss and improved cholesterol levels

Here are some key similarities between the two diets:

- Both diets emphasize whole, nutrient-dense foods, including fruits, vegetables, whole grains, and lean protein.
- Both diets encourage the use of herbs and spices for flavor instead of salt.
- Both diets are associated with improved health outcomes, including lower risk of heart disease and certain types of cancer.

And here are some key differences between the two diets:

- The Mediterranean diet includes more healthy fats, such as olive oil and fatty fish, while the DASH diet is lower in fat overall.
- The DASH diet emphasizes low-fat dairy, while the Mediterranean diet allows for moderate consumption of cheese and yogurt.

- The Mediterranean diet includes moderate consumption of alcohol, particularly red wine, while the DASH diet does not include any alcohol.

While it is possible to incorporate elements of both the Mediterranean and DASH diets into your overall eating pattern, it would be difficult to follow both diets strictly at the same time since they have different recommendations and goals.

The Mediterranean diet emphasizes healthy fats, such as olive oil and fatty fish, and moderate alcohol consumption, while the DASH diet focuses on low-fat dairy and reducing salt intake to lower blood pressure. These differences in recommendations could make it difficult to meet the requirements of both diets simultaneously. Instead of trying to follow both diets at the same time, you could incorporate some of the healthy elements of each into your overall eating pattern. For example, you could emphasize whole, nutrient-dense foods like fruits, vegetables, whole grains, and lean protein, and try to reduce your intake of processed and high-fat foods. You could also aim to use herbs and spices instead of salt for flavor and incorporate some healthy fats, like olive oil, into your cooking. Additionally, you could focus on reducing your intake of saturated and trans fats and choosing low-fat or fat-free dairy options.

Finally, I want to make a comparison with the intermittent fasting method.

The intermittent fasting method:

- Involves cycling between periods of fasting and eating
- Can take many forms, such as the 16/8 method, where you fast for at least 16 hours and eat within an 8-hour window, or the 5:2 method, where you consume your food for 5 days and then decrease your calorie intake to 500-600 calories for 2 days
- Can be done with any type of diet, including the Mediterranean diet
- Associated with weight loss, improved blood sugar control, and other health benefits

Here are some key similarities between the two approaches:

- Both emphasize the importance of eating whole, nutrient-dense foods such as fruits, veggies, whole grains, and lean protein.
- Both have been associated with numerous health benefits, including improved heart health, better blood sugar control, and reduced risk of certain cancers.

And here are some key differences between the two approaches:

- The Mediterranean diet does not require any specific fasting schedule, while intermittent fasting involves specific periods of time when you don't eat.
- The Mediterranean diet focuses on the types of foods you eat, while intermittent fasting focuses on when you eat.

If you do choose to try combining the two approaches, it's important to do so in a way that is healthy and sustainable for you. Here are some tips to consider:

Talk to a healthcare professional: It's important to consult with a healthcare professional before making any major changes to your diet or eating habits, especially if you have any underlying health conditions.

Gradually introduce intermittent fasting: If you're unfamiliar to intermittent fasting, begin carefully and progressively increase the duration of your fasts over time.

Be mindful of nutrient intake: Make sure to focus on consuming nutrient-dense foods during your eating periods to ensure you're getting all the nutrients your body needs.

Stay hydrated: It's essential to drink lot of water during the day, especially during fasting periods.

Listen to your body: Pay attention to how your body feels during the fasting period and adjust your approach as needed.

So in this case it is possible to follow both diets although quite difficult but remember to follow these tips and talk to your doctor regarding intermittent fasting.

Your new shopping list and foods to avoid

Now I want to share your new shopping list of foods that you can easily buy in any grocery store.

Produce:

- Leafy greens such as spinach, kale, and arugula
- Tomatoes
- Cucumbers
- Bell peppers
- Onions
- Garlic
- Zucchini
- Eggplant
- Mushrooms
- Artichokes
- Broccoli
- Cauliflower
- Carrots
- Sweet potatoes
- Avocado
- Lemons

Fruits:

- Berries such as blueberries, raspberries, and strawberries
- Apples
- Oranges
- Grapes
- Melons
- Bananas
- Pears

Protein:

- Fish such as salmon, tuna, and cod
- Shellfish such as shrimp and mussels
- Chicken
- Turkey
- Legumes such as chickpeas, lentils, and black beans
- Nuts and seeds such as almonds, walnuts, pistachios, sunflower seeds, and chia seeds
- Eggs

Dairy:

- Greek yogurt
- Feta cheese
- Parmesan cheese

Grains:

- Whole wheat bread
- Brown rice
- Quinoa
- Whole wheat pasta

Oils and **condiments:**

- Olive oil
- Balsamic vinegar
- Red wine vinegar
- Honey
- Mustard
- Hummus
- Olives

Herbs and **spices:**

- Basil
- Oregano
- Rosemary
- Thyme
- Dill
- Parsley
- Cinnamon
- Cumin
- Paprika

Beans:
- Lentils
- White beans
- Chickpeas
- Butter beans
- Black-eyed peas
- Yellow Split Pea
- Pinto Beans
- Borlotti Beans

This is just a sample shopping list, and you can customize and adapt it based on your preferences and dietary needs.

As for the foods to avoid, the following are:

- Processed and packaged foods: These meals are frequently heavy in added sugars, bad fats, and chemicals. They can also be low in nutrients, so it's best to limit or avoid them.
- Refined grains: Foods made with refined grains such as white bread, pasta, and rice are often low in fiber and nutrients. It's better to choose whole grain options instead.
- Red meat: While red meat can be included in the Mediterranean diet in moderation, it's generally limited in favor of leaner protein sources like fish, chicken, and legumes.
- Sweets and desserts: These foods are typically high in added sugars and can contribute to weight gain and other health problems. Instead of sweets and desserts, try to satisfy your sweet tooth with fresh fruit or a small serving of dark chocolate. Prefer desserts that contain olive oil, not with too much sugar, preferably fruit-based and with ingredients that are as little artificial as possible.
- Processed meats: Processed meats like bacon, sausage, and deli meat are often high in salt, unhealthy fats, and preservatives. They should be limited or avoided.
- Soda and sugary drinks: These drinks are high in added sugars and can develop weight gain and other health issues. It's better to choose water, unsweetened tea, or other low-calorie beverages instead.

Olive oil: its properties and conservation techniques

Olive oil is a type of vegetable oil that is obtained from the fruit of the olive tree. It is commonly used in cooking and as a condiment in many cuisines around the world. Here are some of the properties and benefits of olive oil:

Properties:

- Olive oil is high in monounsaturated fatty acids (MUFA), which are considered healthy fats and have been linked to a reduced risk of heart disease and other chronic conditions.
- It also contains polyphenols, which are natural antioxidants that can protect against stress and inflammation in our body.
- Olive oil has a low smoke point, which means it is not suitable for high heat cooking methods such as deep frying. However, it is great for sautéing, roasting, and baking.

Benefits:

- Consuming olive oil has been linked to a reduced risk of heart disease, stroke, and certain types of cancer.
- It helps improve blood sugar control and insulin sensitivity in individuals with type 2 diabetes.
- Olive oil has anti-inflammatory properties and may help reduce the risk of chronic inflammatory diseases such as rheumatoid arthritis.
- It has also been shown to improve brain function and protect against cognitive decline, especially in older people.

Proper storage is important to maintain the quality of olive oil and prevent it from going rancid or spoiling. Here are some tips on how to keep olive oil:

- Store it in a cool, dark place: Olive oil should be kept in a cool and dark place, away from heat, light, and air. Heat and light can accelerate the oxidation process, which can cause the oil to go rancid. Therefore, it is best to store olive oil in a cool pantry or cupboard away from direct sunlight and heat sources like the stove or oven.
- Keep it in an airtight container: Exposure to air can also cause olive oil to oxidize and lose its flavor and nutritional value. Therefore, it is important to keep the oil in an airtight container to prevent air from getting in. Glass bottles with tight-fitting lids or metal cans are good options for storing olive oil.
- Use it within a reasonable time frame: Olive oil has a shelf life of about 18-24 months from the time of harvest, but this can vary depending on the quality of the oil and the storage conditions. To ensure that the oil stays fresh and flavorful, it is best to use it within a reasonable time frame. Avoid buying large quantities of olive oil that you may not be able to use up before it goes bad.

By following these tips, you can ensure that your olive oil stays fresh and flavorful for as long as possible.

Questions beginners ask most often and answers

Many questions and doubts beginners ask themselves at the beginning of this incredible journey towards the Mediterranean diet. Many are afraid of not making it or not getting the desired results. Clearly like everything, starting a new diet can be difficult at first, but with the advice and recipes in this manual, the path will be gradual and natural. So here are some frequently asked questions that beginners ask themselves.

Is it possible to have snacks on the Mediterranean diet?

Snacking is not discouraged on the Mediterranean diet, but it is important to choose healthy options such as fresh fruit, nuts, or vegetables with hummus. Processed snacks and sugary drinks should be avoided.

Is the Mediterranean diet expensive?

While some specialty ingredients like olives and olive oil may be more expensive, the Mediterranean diet can be affordable and accessible. Choosing seasonal produce, buying in bulk, and preparing meals at home can help save money.

Is it possible to have wine on the Mediterranean diet?

Moderate alcohol consumption, such as a glass of red wine with meals, is a part of the Mediterranean diet for those who choose to drink alcohol. However, excessive alcohol consumption should be avoided for health reasons.

Can the Mediterranean diet followed by vegetarians or vegans?

Yes, the Mediterranean diet can be adjusted to meet the needs of vegetarians or vegans. Plant-based sources of protein such as legumes, nuts, and seeds are encouraged, and dairy and meat can be replaced with plant-based alternatives.

Do I need to count calories on the Mediterranean diet?

The Mediterranean diet does not require calorie counting or strict portion control, but it does emphasize eating a balanced diet of whole foods and limiting processed foods and added sugars. Listening to your body's hunger and fullness cues and eating until you feel satisfied is a key principle of the Mediterranean diet.

How can I begin the Mediterranean diet?

Start by gradually incorporating Mediterranean-style meals and snacks into your diet. Focus on including a variety of colorful fruits and vegetables, whole grains, healthy fats, and lean protein sources. Meal planning and preparation can also help make the Mediterranean diet more manageable and convenient.

Recipes

Breakfast recipes

Greek yogurt scrambled eggs

Servings: 2

Nutrition: 207 Calories, 17g Fat, 13g Protein, 2g Carbohydrates, 130mg Sodium, 330mg Cholesterol

Ingredients:

- Kosher salt
- Extra virgin olive oil
- 4 large eggs
- 1 tablespoon chopped chives
- 2 to 3 tablespoons Greek yogurt

Directions:

1. In a small mixing bowl, combine the eggs and sprinkle generously with kosher salt. Stir in 1 teaspoon olive oil until blended. Set aside 1-2 teaspoons olive oil in a small non-stick pan with a medium-high heat. Heat the olive oil for about 30 seconds before adding the whisked eggs.
2. Fry the eggs over medium heat, whisking constantly with a rubber spatula, until they begin to firm (there will be some wet areas, which is fine).
3. Remove from the heat and stir in the Greek yogurt. Mix until the yogurt is completely blended, and the eggs are completely set. Season with salt and pepper to taste.
4. Place the scrambled eggs on plates and garnish with the chives. Enjoy right away.

Bowl with millet and strawberries

Servings: 4

Nutrition: 360 Calories, 11g Protein, 11g Fat, 55g Carbohydrates, 37mg Sodium, 6mg Cholesterol

Ingredients:

- 1 c. 2% milk, plus more for serving
- 1 c. millet
- 1 1/2 tsp. pure vanilla extract
- 1 lb. strawberries, hulled and halved
- 4 sprigs fresh thyme
- 2 tbsp. finely chopped pistachios
- 2 tbsp. hemp seeds
- 1 tbsp. olive oil
- 1 tbsp. honey

Directions:

1. Preheat the oven to 450°F. Toss strawberries, thyme, oil, and honey on a baking sheet lined with parchment paper. Roast for about 10 minutes, or until the berries start to release juices. Remove from oven and throw away the thyme.
2. Next, bring milk and 1 cup water to a boil in a skillet. Mix millet and vanilla, then decrease heat to low and cover for 25 to 30 minutes, or until millet is soft and liquid is absorbed. End up serving with berries and pan juices, a little of milk, pistachios, and hemp seeds.

Bruschetta with Greek yogurt and tomatoes

Servings: 4

Nutrition: 180 Calories, 8g Protein, 17g Carbohydrates, 10g Fat, 243mg Sodium, 4mg Cholesterol

Ingredients:

- 2 tbsp. olive oil
- 1 tsp. lemon juice
- 1/4 tsp. cumin seed
- 1/4 tsp. ground sumac
- 1/2 c. plain Greek yogurt
- 1 scallion, finely chopped, plus more for serving
- 4 pieces toasted bread
- 3 medium heirloom tomatoes, sliced
- 1/4 c. mint, chopped
- 2 tsp. grated lemon zest
- 1/4 tsp. coarsely cracked pepper
- 1/4 tsp. kosher salt

Directions:

1. Mix Greek yogurt, scallions, mint, and lemon zest in a mixing dish.
2. Stir together the olive oil, lemon juice, cumin seed, ground sumac, roughly cracked pepper, and kosher salt in a separate bowl.
3. Put yogurt on toast, garnish with heirloom tomatoes, then drizzle with vinaigrette. If wanted, top with extra chopped scallions.

Dandelion bruschetta and yogurt

Servings: 4

Nutrition: 300 Calories, 35g Carbohydrates, 14g Fat, 10g Protein, 680mg Sodium, 27mg Cholesterol

Ingredients:

- 1 bunch dandelion greens
- 1/4 tsp. salt
- 1/4 tsp. pepper
- 4 oz. feta cheese
- 2 tbsp. olive oil
- 1 small red onion, thinly sliced
- 1 loaf ciabatta, split and toasted
- 2 tbsp. small mint leaves
- 1/8 tsp. red pepper flakes
- 2 tbsp. lemon juice
- 1/4 c. plain yogurt (not Greek)
- 1 tsp. grated lemon zest

Directions:

1. In a big pan with a medium heat, heat the olive oil. Cook, stirring occasionally, until the red onion and red pepper flakes are just soft, 4 to 5 minutes.
2. Cook until the lemon juice has dissipated, about 30 seconds. Remove from fire, sprinkle with salt and pepper, and mix with dandelion greens (approximately 8 oz., with 5 in. of stem eliminated) until they begin to wilt.
3. Then, in a tiny blender, crumble the feta cheese and pulse four times. With the blender running, combine the yogurt and lemon zest; purée until creamy and silky. (Otherwise, crumble the feta into a mixing bowl and stir in the yogurt and lemon zest.)
4. Distribute on bruschetta, then garnish with greens and mint leaves.

Grain bowl with egg and avocado

Servings: 2

Nutrition: 460 Calories, 15g Protein, 55g Carbohydrates, 20g Fat, 370mg Sodium, 185mg Cholesterol

Ingredients:

- 1 bunch spinach, thick stems discarded, leaves roughly chopped (about 4 cups)
- 1/4 tsp. Kosher salt
- 1/4 tsp. pepper
- 2 c. leftover cooked grains (such as farro, brown rice, quinoa), warmed
- 1/2 avocado, diced
- 1 large eggs
- 1 tbsp. olive oil
- 1 clove garlic, finely chopped
- 1 medium tomato, cut into 1-in. pieces

Directions:

1. Distribute grains among bowls. In a big non-stick saucepan, warm oil and garlic over medium heat for 1 minute, or until garlic begins to turn golden brown. Cook, tossing frequently, until the spinach begins to wilt, 1 to 2 minutes. Serve with tomato and avocado.
2. Return saucepan to medium heat and cook eggs until done to preference, about 2 to 3 minutes for runny yolks. Serve over grain bowls.

Semifreddo with blueberries and dried fruit

Servings: 4

Nutrition: 410 Calories, 22g Protein, 28g Carbohydrates, 26g Fat, 390mg Sodium, 25mg Cholesterol

Ingredients:

- 3 tbsp. pecans
- 3 tbsp. pepitas
- 1 tbsp. olive oil
- 1 tsp. cinnamon
- 1/8 tsp. cardamom
- 1 c. freeze-dried blueberries
- 1 c. water
- 1 pinch of salt
- 1/4 c. golden raisins
- 3 c. Greek yogurt
- 3 tbsp. walnuts
- 3 tbsp. almonds
- 1/2 tsp. flaky sea salt
- 1 tbsp. orange zest

Directions:

1. Blend 1/2 cup freeze-dried blueberries into a powder in a food processor; put to a medium pan. Stir in the water and cook for about 15 minutes, or until the sauce thickens. Mix in a pinch of salt and set aside to cool.
2. Next, stir walnuts, almonds, pecans, and pepitas with olive oil, cinnamon, cardamom, and flaky sea salt. Roast for 6 minutes at 400°F, then stir with orange zest, the remaining 1/2 cup freeze-dried blueberries, and golden raisins.
3. Layer Greek yogurt (3/4 cup each), blueberry sauce (1 Tbsp), and nut mixture (14 cup) to make four semifreddo.

Toast with egg and avocado with oriental flavours

Servings: 2

Nutrition: 450 Calories, 13g Protein, 25g Carbohydrates, 35g Fat, 380mg Sodium, 185mg Cholesterol

Ingredients:	Directions:
<ul><li>2 tsp. fresh lime juice</li><li>Kosher salt</li><li>Pepper</li><li>1/2 tsp. curry powder</li><li>3 tbsp. olive oil, divided</li><li>2 large eggs</li><li>2 tbsp. finely chopped cilantro</li><li>1/2 large avocado</li><li>2 slices whole grain bread, toasted</li></ul>	1. Toast curry powder in a small dry pan with a medium-high heat for 1 minute, or until aromatic. Set aside 2 tablespoons olive oil. 2. Spread avocado on toast with lime juice and a touch of salt. 3. In a medium non-stick pan with a medium-high heat, heat the remaining tbsp. oil. Cook until the whites are golden brown, crisp on the sides, and the yolks are done, about 2 minutes. Remove saucepan from heat and cover until whites are cooked, about 10 seconds, if edges are browned but whites are not set. Sprinkle with pepper and salt to taste.

4. Sprinkle curry oil over each piece of avocado toast and cover with an egg and minced cilantro.

Tender frittata with herbs

Servings: 4

Nutrition: 305 Calories, 12g Protein, 5g Carbohydrates, 26g Fat, 370mg Sodium, 300mg Cholesterol

Ingredients:	Directions:
<ul><li>6 scallions, cut into 1-in. pieces</li><li>2 c. flat-leaf parsley leaves, plus more for sprinkling</li><li>2 c. cilantro leaves and tender stems, plus more for sprinkling</li><li>1/4 c. crème fraîche, at room temp</li><li>2 tbsp. chopped chives</li><li>kosher salt</li><li>pepper</li><li>6 large eggs</li><li>1/2 c. dill fronds, plus more for sprinkling</li><li>4 tbsp. olive oil, divided</li></ul>	1. Preheat the oven to 350°F. Refrigerate the crème fraîche and chives until ready to use. Lightly beat the eggs in a bowl. In a blender, combine scallions, parsley, cilantro, dill, and 2 tablespoons oil and pulse until evenly and finely chopped. Mix in a mixing dish with the eggs and 1/2 teaspoon salt and pepper. Heat the remaining 2 tablespoons oil in a medium saucepan on a low flame until shimmering, about 2 minutes. Cook until the edges of the egg mixture begin to sizzle and set, about 2 minutes. Put the pan in the oven and cook for 18 to 20 minutes, or until center is just set. Rest for at least 5 minutes. Serve with chive crème fraîche. If desired, top with more herbs.

Avocado Cheese Omelette

Servings: 2

Nutrition: 350 Calories, 32g Protein, 10g Carbohydrates, 22g Fat, 300mg Sodium, 200mg Cholesterol

Ingredients:

- 1 c. baby spinach
- 4 large eggs plus 2 egg whites
- 2 oz. sharp Cheddar, coarsely grated
- 1 tsp. olive oil
- 1 small red onion, finely chopped
- 1/4 c. fresh flat-leaf parsley, chopped
- 1/2 small avocado
- Kosher salt and pepper
- 6 cremini mushrooms, sliced
- 1 c. grape tomatoes, halved

Directions:

1. In a large non-stick pan with a medium heat, heat the oil. Sprinkle the onion with 1/4 teaspoon salt and pepper and simmer for 4 minutes, turning regularly. Cook, stir to combine, until the mushrooms are cooked, about 4 minutes. Toss in the spinach and simmer until it begins to wilt.
2. Whisk in the eggs for 1 minute, then cook without shaking for 2 to 3 minutes, or until the edges are golden. Top with cheese and fold in half to form a semi-circle.
3. Mix tomatoes, parsley, and avocado together and spoon over omelette.

Nectarine peach bruschetta

Servings: 2

Nutrition: 480 Calories, 10g Protein, 35g Carbohydrates, 35g Fat, 303mg Sodium, 20mg Cholesterol

Ingredients:

- 1/4 c. olive oil
- 2 tsp. very coarsely cracked black pepper
- 1 1/2 tbsp. white wine vinegar
- 1 tsp. honey
- 1/3 c. fresh ricotta cheese
- 2 slices of bread
- 1 nectarine, sliced

Directions:

1. To melt, stir together white wine vinegar and honey in a mixing dish. Toss in the nectarine and let aside for 10 minutes to marinate. Mix with olive oil and black pepper to coat.
2. Put ricotta on grilled or toasted bread, then top with nectarines and juices.

Bruschetta with spinach, squash and egg

Servings: 4

Nutrition: 265 Calories, 13g Protein, 20g Carbohydrates, 14g Fat, 420mg Sodium, 193mg Cholesterol

Ingredients:
- 1 bunch spinach, roughly chopped
- 1/4 tsp. salt
- 1/4 tsp. pepper
- 1 large butternut squash
- 1 tbsp. oil
- 1/3 c. Gruyère cheese
- 4 eggs
- 2 cloves garlic, chopped
- 4 pieces bread

Directions:

1. Remove the neck from the butternut squash, peel and slice into half-inch chunks.
2. Sauté for eight minutes, covered, in a non-stick pan with oil, stirring frequently. Cook, stirring occasionally, until the squash is golden brown and soft. Add pepper and salt to taste and toss with spinach.
3. Toast the bread and top with Gruyère cheese.
4. When bread is being topped with cooked squash, fry an egg and add one to each piece when finished.

Nutritious spinach crepes

Servings: 6

Nutrition: 327 Calories, 13g Protein, 47g Carbohydrates, 11g Fat, 540mg Sodium, 2 mg Cholesterol

Ingredients:
- 3 tbsp. safflower oil
- 3/4 tsp. kosher salt
- 1 sm yellow onion, chopped
- 1 can (15.5 oz) chickpeas, rinsed and drained
- 1 granny smith apple, diced
- 2 lg eggs
- 1/3 C finely chopped fresh cilantro
- 10 oz. fresh spinach
- lemon wedges, for serving
- 2 1/2 C 1% milk
- 1 C plus 2 tbsp all-purpose flour
- 1/4 C golden raisins
- 2 tbsp. madras curry powder
- 1/4 tsp. black pepper

Directions:

1. In a processor, combine the eggs, cilantro, pepper, 1 cup each of milk and flour, 2 tablespoons oil, and 1/4 teaspoon salt. Lightly coat non-stick saucepan with cooking spray and heat over medium heat. Spoon 1/3 cup batter into pan and heat until edges are firm, about 1 minute. Cook for 30 seconds on the other side. Repeat with the remaining crepes. Keep warm by covering.
2. In a pan, heat the remaining 1 tablespoon oil over medium heat. Cook until the onion is tender, about 5 minutes. Combine the chickpeas, apple, raisins, and curry powder in a mixing bowl. Cook for 3 minutes. Cook for 30 seconds after adding the remaining 2 tablespoons flour. Add in the remaining 1 1/2 cups milk. Simmer for 2 minutes, or until the sauce is thick. Stir in the spinach and the remaining 1/2 teaspoon salt. Sauté for 2 minutes, or until wilted. Distribute the filling among the crepes, fold in half, and garnish with lemon wedges.

Bruschetta with feta cheese and watermelon radishes

Servings: 4

Nutrition: 275 Calories, 37g Carbohydrates, 11g Protein, 9f Fat, 675mg Sodium, 20mg Cholesterol

Ingredients:

- 1 medium watermelon radish, very thinly sliced
- 2 red radishes, very thinly sliced
- 1/2 c. radish or broccoli sprouts
- 3 oz. feta cheese, broken into pieces
- 2 tbsp. milk
- kosher salt, for serving
- pepper, for serving
- 4 thick slices sourdough toast
- olive oil, for serving

Directions:

1. Mash feta cheese and milk in a tiny blender until smooth, adding extra milk if needed. Spread on slices of bread. Garnish with watermelon radish, red radishes,radish and broccoli sprouts. Sprinkle with olive oil and season with salt and pepper to taste.

Nutritious bowl with blueberries, dried fruits and granola

Servings: 2

Nutrition: 370 Calories, 25g Protein, 32g Carbohydrates, 17g Fat, 130mg Sodium, 0mg Cholesterol

Ingredients:

- 1 tsp. pure vanilla extract
- 1/2 c. fresh blueberries
- 1/4 c. vanilla granola
- 1 c. frozen blueberries
- 1/2 c. unsweetened almond milk
- 2 tsp hemp seeds
- 1 tsp ground cinnamon
- 1 1/2 scoops protein powder
- 2 tbsp. unsweetened almond butter
- 2 tbsp sliced almonds

Directions:

1. Mash frozen blueberries, almond milk, protein powder, almond butter, and vanilla in a food processor until smooth. Split the mixture between two bowls.
2. Before serving, garnish each bowl with fresh blueberries, granola, almonds, hemp seeds, and cinnamon.

Bowl of oats with banana and chocolate

Servings: 1

Nutrition: 295 Calories, 7g Protein, 50g Carbohydrates, 8g Fat, 230mg Sodium, 10mg Cholesterol

Ingredients:

- ½ cup old-fashioned rolled oats
- ½ small banana, sliced
- 1 cup water
- Pinch of salt
- 1 tablespoon chocolate-hazelnut spread
- Pinch of flaky sea salt

Directions:

1. In a medium pan, bring water and a pinch of normal salt to a boil. Toss in the oats, decrease the heat to medium, and cook, stirring frequently, for about 5 minutes, or until most of the liquid has been absorbed. Remove from the heat, cover, and let aside for 2 to 3 minutes. Garnish with sliced bananas, chocolate spread, and flaky salt.

Pasta and Rice Entrées

Pasta with tomato and basil

Servings: 4

Nutrition: 340 Calories, 11g Protein, 55g Carbohydrates, 10g Fat, 460mg Sodium

Ingredients:

- 1 ½ teaspoons Italian seasoning
- ½ teaspoon onion powder
- ½ teaspoon garlic powder
- ½ teaspoon salt
- ¼ teaspoon crushed red pepper
- 8 ounces whole-wheat rotini
- 1 cup water
- ½ cup slivered basil
- Grated Parmesan cheese for garnish
- 2 cups low-sodium "no-chicken" broth or chicken broth
- 1 (15 ounce) can no-salt-added diced tomatoes
- 2 tablespoons extra-virgin olive oil
- 6 cups baby kale or baby spinach

Directions:

1. In a big saucepan, mix the pasta, water, broth, tomatoes, oil, Italian seasoning, onion powder, garlic powder, salt, and crushed red pepper. Bring to a boil, covered, over high heat. Uncover, decrease heat to medium-high, and cook for 10 minutes, stirring constantly. Cook, stirring frequently, till most of the liquid has been evaporated, 5 to 7 minutes more. (If using spinach, add it after about 10 minutes so it may finish cooking in the last 2 to 3 minutes.) Stir in the basil. If preferred, sprinkle with Parmesan.

Traditional Chicken Parmesan pasta

Servings: 4

Nutrition: 540 Calories, 42g Protein, 56g Carbohydrates, 17g Fat, 610mg Sodium, 74mg Cholesterol

Ingredients:

- 1 teaspoon Italian seasoning
- ¼ teaspoon salt
- 3 cups low-sodium chicken broth
- 1 ½ cups crushed tomatoes
- 2 tablespoons extra-virgin olive oil, divided
- ¼ cup whole-wheat panko breadcrumbs
- ¼ cup shredded Parmesan cheese
- ¼ cup chopped fresh basil
- 1 tablespoon plus 1 teaspoon minced garlic, divided
- 1 pound boneless, skinless chicken breast, cut into 1/2-inch pieces
- 8 ounces whole-wheat penne
- ½ cup shredded mozzarella cheese

Directions:

1. In a large ovenproof pan with a medium-high heat, warm 1 tablespoon oil. Mix in the panko and 1 teaspoon garlic. Sauté, stirring constantly, for 1 to 2 minutes, or until the panko is golden brown. Place in a small bowl and put aside. Clean the pan clean.
2. In the pan, cook the remaining 1 tablespoon oil over medium-high heat. Combine the chicken, Italian seasoning, salt, and the other 1 tablespoon garlic in a mixing bowl. Sauté, stirring regularly, for about 2 minutes, or until the chicken is no longer pink on the exterior. Add in the tomatoes, penne, and broth. Bring to a boil and cook, uncovered, for 15 to 20 minutes, or until the penne is tender and the sauce has decreased and thickened.
3. In the meantime, place an oven rack in the upper third of the oven. Turn on the broiler to high. When the pasta is done, top it with the mozzarella mixture. Put the pan to the broiler for 1 minute, or until the mozzarella is bubbling and beginning to brown. Serve with the panko mixture, Parmesan, and basil on top.

Greek pasta with feta

Servings: 4

Nutrition: 488 Calories, 23g Protein, 60g Carbohydrates, 20g fat, 622mg Sodium, 62mg Cholesterol

Ingredients:

- 1 (8 ounce) can no-salt-added tomato sauce
- 4 cups lightly packed baby spinach (half of a 5-ounce box)
- 6 cups cooked whole-wheat rotini pasta
- ¼ cup chopped pitted Kalamata olives
- 2 tablespoons olive oil
- 3 links cooked chicken sausage (9 ounces), sliced into rounds
- 2 tablespoons olive oil
- ½ cup finely crumbled feta cheese
- ¼ cup chopped fresh basil
- 1 cup diced onion
- 1 clove garlic, minced

Directions:

1. In a big skillet, heat the oil over medium-high heat. Cook, turning frequently, until the sausage, onion, and garlic begin to brown, 4 to 6 minutes. Cook, stirring frequently, until the tomato sauce is steaming hot, and the spinach has wilted, 3 to 5 minutes. If required, add 1 to 2 tablespoons water to keep the pasta from adhering. Stir in the feta and basil.

Vegetarian fettuccine with mushrooms

Servings: 6

Nutrition: 385 Calories, 19g Protein, 56g Carbohydrates, 10g Fat, 430mg Sodium, 20mg Cholesterol

Ingredients:

- 1 tablespoon minced garlic
- 2 tablespoons sherry vinegar
- 2 cups low-fat milk
- 2 tablespoons all-purpose flour
- 12 ounces whole-wheat fettuccine
- 1 tablespoon extra-virgin olive oil
- ½ teaspoon freshly ground pepper
- 1 cup finely shredded Asiago cheese, plus more for garnish
- 4 cups sliced mixed mushrooms, such as cremini, oyster and/or shiitake
- 4 cups thinly sliced Brussels sprouts
- ½ teaspoon salt

Directions:

1. Boil pasta in a large saucepan of boiling water for 8 to 10 minutes, or until soft. Return to the pan and set aside after draining.
2. Next, in a big saucepan with a medium heat, heat the oil. Toss in the mushrooms and Brussels sprouts and cook for 8 to 10 minutes, or until the mushrooms lose their juice. Sauté, stirring frequently, for approximately 1 minute, or until the garlic is fragrant. Scrape up any brown parts with the sherry (or vinegar); bring to a boil and cook, whisking, until almost absorbed, 10 seconds.
3. In a mixing dish, combine the milk and flour, season with salt and pepper. Simmer, stirring constantly, for about 2 minutes, or until the sauce bubbles and thickens. Add Asiago and stir until melted.
4. Gently mix the pasta in the sauce. If wanted, top with more cheese.

Pesto pasta with asparagus and chicken

Servings: 6

Nutrition: 423 Calories, 32g Protein, 32g Carbohydrates, 18g Fat, 712mg Sodium, 70mg Cholesterol

Ingredients:

- 1 (7 ounce) container refrigerated basil pesto
- 1 teaspoon salt
- ¼ teaspoon ground pepper
- 8 ounces whole-wheat penne
- 1 pound fresh asparagus, trimmed and cut into 2-inch pieces
- 1 ounce Parmesan cheese, grated (about 1/4 cup)
- Small fresh basil leaves for garnish
- 3 cups shredded cooked chicken breast

Directions:

1. Cook pasta following package instructions in a large saucepan. During the last 2 minutes of cooking, add the asparagus to the saucepan. Save 1/2 cup cooking water after draining.
2. Return the spaghetti to the pot and whisk in the chicken, pesto, salt, and pepper. Add 1 tablespoon at a time, mix in the remaining cooking water to get the desired consistency. Move the mixture to a dish and top with Parmesan and basil, if wanted. Serve right away.

Vegetarian ravioli with artichokes

Servings: 4

Nutrition: 450 Calories, 15g Protein, 61g Carbohydrates, 19g Fat, 700mg Sodium, 20mg Cholesterol

Ingredients:

- 1 (10 ounce) package frozen quartered artichoke hearts, thawed
- 1 (15 ounce) can no-salt-added cannellini beans, rinsed
- 2 (8 ounce) packages frozen or refrigerated spinach-and-ricotta ravioli
- ½ cup oil-packed sun-dried tomatoes, drained (2 tablespoons oil reserved)
- 3 tablespoons toasted pine nuts
- ¼ cup chopped fresh basil
- ¼ cup Kalamata olives, sliced

Directions:

1. A large pot of water should be brought to a boil. Cook the ravioli following the package instructions. Set aside after draining and tossing with 1 tablespoon leftover oil.
2. In a big non-stick pan with a medium-high heat, heat the remaining 1 tablespoon oil. Sauté the artichokes and beans for 2 to 3 minutes, or until warmed through.
3. Combine the cooked ravioli, sun-dried tomatoes, olives, pine nuts, and basil in a mixing bowl.

Tomato macaroni with fresh ricotta

Servings: 6

Nutrition: 360 Calories, 14g Protein, 47g Carbohydrates, 12g fat, 445mg Sodium, 15mg Cholesterol

Ingredients:

- ¼ teaspoon ground pepper
- ⅛ teaspoon salt plus 1 tablespoon, divided
- 12 ounces thin tube-shaped pasta
- 2 tablespoons extra-virgin olive oil
- 6 tablespoons finely chopped yellow onion
- 10 fresh basil leaves, thinly sliced
- ¼ cup freshly grated Parmigiano-Reggiano cheese
- 6 ounces mild pork sausage, casings removed
- 1 14-ounce can no-salt-added whole peeled tomatoes, chopped, with their juice
- 6 tablespoons part-skim ricotta cheese

Directions:

1. In a big pot, bring 2 quarts of water to a boil.
2. Next, in a large pan with a medium-high heat, add the oil, onion, and sausage. 4 to 5 minutes, tossing and breaking the sausage with a spoon, until the onion is brown. Cook, stirring occasionally, until the tomatoes have softened, about 5 to 10 minutes. Take the pan off the heat.
3. Put the remaining 1 tablespoon salt to the boiling water, mix in the pasta, and cook until just cooked, according to package directions.
4. Bring the sauce to a medium-low heat just before the pasta is cooked. Stir in the ricotta and basil until well mixed. Drain the pasta well and combine with the sauce and Parmigiano. Serve.

Delicious pasta with cherry tomatoes

Servings: 4

Nutrition: 385 Calories, 16g Protein, 48g Carbohydrates, 15g Fat, 620mg Sodium, 24mg Cholesterol

Ingredients:
- 2 cups cherry tomatoes
- 1 medium yellow squash, halved and sliced 1/4 inch thick
- ¾ teaspoon salt
- 8 ounces whole-wheat penne pasta
- 2 tablespoons extra-virgin olive oil
- 1 cup pearl-size or mini mozzarella balls (about 4 ounces)
- ¼ cup finely grated Parmesan cheese
- 6 cloves garlic, peeled
- 1 cup chopped fresh basil

Directions:

1. A big pot of water should be brought to a boil. Put pasta and cook following package guidelines. Save aside 1/4 cup of the cooking water, then drain the pasta and cover to keep hot.
2. Next, in a big non-stick pan with a medium-high heat, heat the oil. Turn the heat to medium and cook, whisking constantly, until garlic softens and turns light golden, about 3 minutes. Cook, tossing frequently, until the squash is tender, and the tomatoes start to burst, about 4 to 5 minutes. Mash the garlic gently with the back of a spoon. Take the pan off the heat.
3. Mix in the pasta and saved boiling water, as well as the basil and mozzarella. Serve with Parmesan cheese on top.

Summer pasta salad

Servings: 1

Nutrition: 505 Calories, 33g Protein, 38g Carbohydrates, 24g Fat, 740mg Sodium, 33mg Cholesterol

Ingredients:
- ½ cup canned quartered artichoke hearts, drained and cut in half
- 1 cup lightly packed baby kale
- 4 pitted Kalamata olives, roughly chopped
- 1 (3 ounce) can no-salt-added light tuna in water, drained
- 2 tablespoons plain hummus
- 1 tablespoon water
- 1 tablespoon toasted chopped walnuts
- 1 tablespoon Juice from 1/4 lemon
- 2 teaspoons extra-virgin olive oil
- ½ cup chopped red bell pepper
- ½ cup cooked farfalle, preferably whole-wheat
- 1 tablespoon crumbled feta cheese

Directions:

1. In a small mixing bowl, combine the hummus and water. Set aside.
2. In a medium non-stick pan with a medium-high heat, heat the oil. Cook for 1 minute after adding the bell pepper. Mix in the artichoke hearts, greens, and olives. Carefully toss in the tuna, being careful not to break it up too much; simmer until the tuna is heated through, about 1 minute more. Mix in the pasta. Take off the heat and combine with the hummus sauce. If wanted, garnish with feta and walnuts and sprinkle with lemon juice.

Pesto pasta with vegetables

Servings: 5

Nutrition: 315 Calories, 8g Protein, 38g Carbohydrates, 15g Fat, 470mg Sodium, 5mg Cholesterol

Ingredients:

- ¼ cup grated Parmesan cheese
- 2 tablespoons mayonnaise
- 2 tablespoons extra-virgin olive oil
- 2 tablespoons lemon juice
- 8 ounces whole-wheat fusilli (about 3 cups)
- 1 cup small broccoli florets
- ½ teaspoon ground pepper
- 1 cup quartered cherry tomatoes
- 2 cups packed fresh basil leaves
- ¼ cup pine nuts, toasted
- 1 large clove garlic, quartered
- ¾ teaspoon salt

Directions:

1. Warm up a big pot of water. Cook fusilli following per package instructions. Toss in broccoli one minute before the pasta is cooked. Cook for 1 minute before draining and rinsing under cold running water to end the cooking process.
2. Next, in a little blender, combine basil, pine nuts, Parmesan, mayonnaise, oil, lemon juice, garlic, salt, and pepper. Process until nearly creamy. Add to a large mixing bowl. Combine the pasta, broccoli, and tomatoes in a mixing bowl. To coat, toss with a fork.

Greek rice with black beans

Servings: 8

Nutrition: 200 Calories, 5g Fat, 30g Carbohydrates, 8g Protein, 160mg Sodium, 2mg Cholesterol

Ingredients:

- 1/2 tsp turmeric
- 1/2 tsp smoked paprika
- 1/2 tsp cayenne pepper
- 1 3/4 cups chicken or vegetable stock
- 1 can (30 oz) chickpeas, drained and rinsed
- 1/2 cup Greek yogurt
- 1 bunch scallions, chopped
- 2 tbsp. olive oil
- 6 cloves garlic, minced
- 1/2 lemon juice
- 1 tomato, chopped or cut into thin slices
- 1 cup uncooked basmati rice
- 1/4 tsp salt
- 1/2 tsp cumin
- 1 can (30 oz) black beans, drained and rinsed
- 1 bunch parsley, chopped

Directions:

1. In a big skillet over medium heat, heat the olive oil. Cook for 1 minute after adding the garlic.
2. Combine rice, salt, cumin, sumac (optional), turmeric, paprika, and cayenne pepper in a mixing bowl. Boil and stir for 5 minutes, then add chicken stock.
3. Bring the water to a boil. Lower the heat to low, cover, and leave to simmer for 20 minutes.
4. Carefully fold in the chickpeas, black beans, parsley, and lemon juice.
5. Cook for 5 minutes more on low heat.
6. Top with whole parsley leaves, tomatoes, scallions, and a scoop of Greek yogurt.

Greek rice with lemon

Servings: 6

Nutrition: 145 Calories, 7g Fat, 4g Protein, 19g Carbohydrates, 53mg Sodium

Ingredients:

- 1 garlic clove, minced
- ½ cup orzo pasta
- 2 lemons, juice of (and zest of 1 lemon)
- 2 cups long grain rice
- extra virgin olive oil
- Large handful chopped fresh parsley
- 1 tsp dill weed
- 1 medium yellow onion, chopped
- 2 cups low sodium broth
- Pinch salt

Directions:

1. Rinse the rice thoroughly before soaking it in cold water for 15 to 20 minutes. You should be able to shatter it by simply placing a grain of rice between your index and middle fingers. Drain completely.
2. In a big saucepan pan with a lid, heat about 3 tablespoons extra virgin olive oil until it is shimmering but not smoking. Cook for 3 to 4 minutes, or until the onions are transparent. Garlic and orzo pasta are optional. Toss for a few minutes until the orzo has developed some color, then mix in the rice. To coat, toss with a fork.
3. Now stir in the lemon juice and broth. Bring the liquid to a boil (it should reduce slightly), then lower to a low heat. Cook for about 20 minutes, or until the rice is done. The liquid should be completely absorbed, and the rice should be soft.
4. Take the rice from the heat. Let it covered and undisturbed for around 10 minutes for best effects.
5. Remove the lid and mix in the parsley, dill weed, and lemon zest. Garnish with a few slices of lemon, if desired. Enjoy!

Mediterranean brown rice

Servings: 10

Nutrition: 123 Calories, 17g Carbohydrates, 6g Fat, 2g Protein, 190mg Sodium

Ingredients:

- 1 cup Brown Rice long grain
- 2 cups Vegetable Broth
- 1 teaspoon Turmeric
- 2 Tablespoons Olive Oil
- ½ Yellow Onion finely chopped
- Black Pepper to taste
- ¼ cup Pine Nuts toasted
- 3 cloves Garlic minced
- ¼ teaspoon Oregano
- ¼ teaspoon Cumin

Directions:

1. Cook the onion for 2 minutes in a medium skillet with olive oil over medium heat.
2. Cook for another minute after adding the garlic.
3. Combine the rice, broth, and spices in a mixing bowl. Bring to a boil, then remove from the heat. Lower the heat to low and continue to cook for 35-40 minutes, or until all of the broth has been evaporated.
4. Remove from the heat and let aside for 10 minutes, covered. Remove the cover and fluff with a fork before stirring in the toasted pine nuts.

Fried rice with feta

Servings: 4

Nutrition: 205 Calories, 6g Protein, 27g Carbohydrates, 8g Fat, 223mg Sodium, 17mg Cholesterol

Ingredients:
- 2 cups brown rice cooked
- 2 roma tomatoes diced small
- 1 tablespoon olive oil
- 1/4 cup red onion minced
- 2 cups baby spinach fresh
- 1/2 cup fat-free feta cheese crumbled
- 2 cloves garlic minced

Directions:

1. In a big pan with a medium heat, warm the olive oil. When the oil is hot, add the onion and garlic and sauté until the onion becomes translucent. Turn the heat up to medium-high and add the rice.
2. Cook the rice for 5 minutes, or until it is hot. Mix in the tomatoes and spinach and simmer, stirring frequently, until the spinach has wilted. Remove from the heat and stir in the feta cheese gradually. Serve immediately.

Traditional tomato rice

Servings: 4

Nutrition: 295 Calories, 7g Fat, 52g Carbohydrates, 5g Protein, 60mg Sodium, 0mg Cholesterol

Ingredients:
- 1 teaspoon dried thyme
- 1/2 teaspoon dried marjoram
- 1 cup diced green bell pepper
- 1 (15 ounce) can tomatoes, drained and reserve liquid
- 1 cup chopped onion
- 2 garlic cloves, minced
- salt and pepper
- 3 cups cooked rice
- 2 tablespoons olive oil
- 1 cup thinly sliced celery
- 1 tablespoon tomato paste

Directions:

1. Cook the onions and garlic in oil in a big pan on a low flame for 5 minutes, stirring constantly.
2. Cook and stir for 2 minutes more after adding the celery, thyme, and marjoram.
3. Cook and stir for another 2-3 minutes after adding the bell pepper.
4. Stir in the drained tomatoes and tomato paste, smashing the tomatoes as you go.
5. Season with salt and pepper to taste.
6. Mix in the rice until well combined.
7. If the mixture is too dry, add some of the conserved tomato liquid until the required consistency is reached.
8. The dish is ready to serve when the rice is warm.

Basmati rice with herbs

Servings: 6

Nutrition: 170 Calories, 3g Fat, 27g Carbohydrates, 4g Protein, 207mg Sodium, 0mg Cholesterol

Ingredients:

- 1/2 cup chopped celery
- 8 ounces button mushrooms, sliced
- 2 garlic cloves, minced (or more or less, to suit)
- 1 tablespoon olive oil
- 1 3/4 cups water
- 1 teaspoon low-sodium instant chicken bouillon granules
- 1/2 teaspoon salt
- 1/4 teaspoon ground black pepper
- 1 cup basmati rice
- 1/2 cup chopped onion
- 2 tablespoons snipped fresh herbs
- 1 teaspoon snipped fresh rosemary

Directions:

1. Bring water to a boil in a large skillet; mix in the bouillon. Toss in the rice many times until it returns to a boil. Turn the heat down low. Cover the pan and allow it to simmer for about 10 minutes, or until the liquid has been absorbed. Take the saucepan from the heat and let it aside, covered, for 10 minutes. Do not remove the cover.
2. Next, cook the celery, onion, garlic, and mushrooms in the olive oil in a big pan on a medium-high heat for 3 minutes, or until the celery and onion are soft. Turn off the heat in the pan.

Mediterranean rice with chicken powder

Servings: 5

Nutrition: 410 Calories, 7g Fat, 80g Carbohydrates, 7g Protein, 17mg Sodium, 0mg Cholesterol

Ingredients:

- 2 cups rice
- 2 teaspoons chicken stock powder
- 2 tablespoons lemon rind, grated
- 2 tablespoons olive oil
- 1 onion, finely chopped
- black pepper
- boiling water
- 1 garlic clove, crushed
- 1/4 cup parsley, chopped

Directions:

1. Warm the oil and sauté the onion and garlic until soft, then toss in the rice.
2. Pour in hot water until the pan is 3/4 full. Bring to a boil, stirring constantly.
3. Stir in the stock and bring to a boil for 10-12 minutes, or until the vegetables are cooked. Drain well.
4. Return to the pan and mix in the lemon peel, parsley, and pepper to incorporate.

Yummy rice with shrimps

Servings: 4

Nutrition: 480 Calories, 16g Fat, 62g Carbohydrates, 23g Protein, 170mg Sodium, 130mg Cholesterol

Ingredients:

- 4 -5 tablespoons extra virgin olive oil
- 4 ripe tomatoes, seeded and diced
- 1 large fennel bulb, halved, cored and cut into ¼ inch dice
- 1 1/4 cups arborio rice or 1 1/4 cups long-grain white rice
- 1/4 cup fresh lemon juice
- 1/4 cup chopped fresh dill
- 1 clove garlic, minced
- 3/4 lb shrimp, shelled and deveined
- 4 scallions, thinly sliced

Directions:

1. Bring 10 cups of water to a boil in a big pot.
2. Add 1 tbsp salt and mix well.
3. Cook, uncovered, over medium heat until the rice is al dente, about 15 minutes.
4. Drain in a colander, then rinse with cold water and drain once more.
5. In a big bowl, put the rice.
6. Bring a pot of salted water to a boil, then add 1 tablespoon lemon juice.
7. Cook until the shrimp are opaque, about 12 minutes.
8. The shrimp should be drained.
9. Move to a cutting board and cut into small pieces.
10. Mix the rice with the 14-cup oil and the remaining 3 tablespoons lemon juice.
11. Toss in the shrimp, tomatoes, fennel, onions, dill, and garlic.
12. Put up to 1 tablespoon additional oil.
13. Add a pinch of salt and crushed red pepper flakes to taste.
14. Enjoy.

Traditional Italian rice salad

Servings: 4

Nutrition: 430 Calories, 9g Fat, 76g Carbohydrates, 10g Protein, 425mg Sodium, 0mg Cholesterol

Ingredients:

- 5/8 cup seeded tomatoes, chopped
- 1/3 cup onion, chopped
- 1 3/4 cups brown rice, cooked
- 1 (8 5/8 ounce) can black beans, drained, rinsed
- 1/4 cup fresh parsley, chopped
- 1/2 cup Italian dressing

Directions:

1. In a small bowl, stir all ingredients except the dressing.
2. Mix in the dressing to coat.
3. Keep it in the fridge for a minimum of 3 hours before serving.

Rice salad with salmon

Servings: 4

Nutrition: 630 Calories, 15g Fat, 100g Carbohydrates, 22g protein, 73mg Sodium, 28mg Cholesterol

Ingredients:

- 250 g rice
- 125 g green beans
- 250 g salmon
- 50 ml oil
- 1/4 cucumber
- 7 1/2 g dill
- 1 lemon
- 1/2 tablespoon mustard

Directions:

1. Set the oven temperature to 360 F. Place the salmon on a big piece of foil and sprinkle with 1 tablespoon of oil and a squeeze of lemon. To construct a sealed parcel, fold up the sides of the foil. Place the fish on a baking sheet and bake for 20 minutes, or until cooked through.
2. Next, cook the rice according to package directions. Next, set aside to cool. Bring a pot of water to a boil, then add the beans and cook for 3 minutes before draining and refreshing in cool water.
3. In a jug, combine the remaining oil, lemon juice, mustard, and most of the dill to create a dressing. Pour the dressing over the rice, beans, and cucumber in a bowl. Mix the salmon with the rice, keeping a little extra for dishing. Serve with the leftover salmon and dill on top.

Seafood, meat and poultry entrées

Delicious cod with lemon

Servings: 5

Nutrition: 320 Calories, 10g Carbohydrates, 26g Protein, 20g Fat, 460mg Sodium, 70mg Cholesterol

Ingredients:

- 5 tbsp extra virgin olive oil
- 2 tablespoons melted butter
- 1.5 lb Cod fillet pieces, 4-6 pieces
- ¼ cup chopped fresh parsley leaves
- 5 garlic cloves, minced
- 5 tablespoon fresh lemon juice
- ¾ teaspoon sweet Spanish paprika
- ¾ teaspoon ground cumin
- ⅓ cup all-purpose flour
- 1 teaspoon ground coriander
- ¾ teaspoon salt
- ½ teaspoon black pepper

Directions:

1. Preheat the oven to 400°F.
2. In a small bowl, combine the lemon juice, olive oil, and melted butter (do not put the garlic yet). Set aside.
3. Combine the all-purpose flour, spices, salt, and pepper in a separate shallow basin. Serve alongside the lemon sauce.
4. Clean the fish with a paper towel. Dip the fish first in the lemon sauce, then in the flour mixture. Remove any extra flour. Save the lemon sauce aside for later.
5. Preheat a cast-iron pan in a saucepan. Add 2 tablespoon olive oil, heated over medium-high. Keep an eye on the oil to ensure it is shimmering but not burning. Sear the salmon on each side to give it color, but do not completely cook (approximately 2 minutes on each side). Remove the pan from heat.
6. Mix the chopped garlic into the leftover lemon sauce. Sprinkle over the fillets of fish.
7. Bake until the fish flakes lightly with a fork in a hot oven. Take it out of the oven and top with parsley. Serve right away.

Nutritious halibut with veggies

Servings: 6

Nutrition: 310 Calories, 11g Carbohydrates, 20g Fat, 23g Protein, 470mg Sodium, 55mg Cholesterol

Ingredients:

- 1 ½ tablespoon freshly minced garlic
- 2 teaspoon dill weed
- 1 teaspoon seasoned salt, more for later
- Zest of 2 lemons
- Juice of 2 lemons
- 1 teaspoon dried oregano
- ½ to ¾ teaspoon ground coriander
- 1 cup extra virgin olive oil
- ½ teaspoon ground black pepper
- 1 pound cherry tomatoes
- 1 large yellow onion, sliced into half moons
- 1-pound fresh green beans
- 1 ½ pound halibut fillet, slice into 1 ½-inch pieces

Directions:

1. Set the oven temperature to 425 degrees Fahrenheit.
2. Mix together the first 9 ingredients in a big mixing bowl. Stir in the green beans, tomatoes, and onions to cover with the sauce. Put the veggies to a large baking tray using a slotted spoon. Place the vegetables to one side of the baking sheet and distribute them out in a single layer.
3. Stir the halibut fillet strips in the leftover sauce to coat. Place the halibut fillet on top of the vegetables on the baking sheet and drizzle with any residual sauce.
4. Sprinkle the halibut and veggies lightly with extra seasoned salt.
5. Bake for 15 minutes at 425°F in a preheated oven. Then, carefully move the baking sheet to the top oven rack and cook for another 5 minutes. Under the broiler, the cherry tomatoes should start to pop.
6. Remove the cooked halibut and vegetables from the oven when they are done. Serve right away.

Gourmet chicken with veggies

Servings: 5

Nutrition: 680 Calories, 7g Fat, 64g Carbohydrates, 48g Protein, 163mg Cholesterol, 140mg Sodium

Ingredients:

- 6 oz bulk Chorizo sausage
- 1 large green bell pepper cored, chopped
- 1 medium red onion peeled, chopped
- 2 garlic cloves peeled, crushed
- 1 ½ cup medium grain rice washed
- 4 bone-in skin-on chicken thighs
- 3 tablespoon tomato paste
- 3 cups chicken broth
- 4 chicken drumsticks
- Olive oil
- 1 large ripe tomato chopped
- 1 teaspoon salt
- 1 teaspoon black pepper
- 1 tablespoon smoked paprika
- 1 teaspoon garlic powder

Directions:

1. Put the rice in a bowl after thoroughly rinsing it. Let the rice to soak in water for 15 minutes while you work on the other ingredients. You should be able to easily break a grain of rice. Drain thoroughly.
2. Prepare the spice rub. Combine the spices, salt, and pepper in a mixing bowl. Wipe the chicken and season with the spice rub, lifting the skins and sprinkling some spice rub below. Put 1 tablespoon extra-virgin olive oil, heated in a 5-quart braiser pan over moderate flame until shimmering but not burning. Add the chicken and brown it thoroughly on both sides.
3. Take the chicken and place it on a platter for the time being. Add the chorizo to the same pan. Simmer for 10 minutes, stirring frequently, until the chorizo has browned well. Combine the green peppers, onions, and garlic in a mixing bowl. Cook for 5 minutes, stirring often, over medium heat. Put also the diced tomatoes, tomato paste, and chicken broth. Transfer the browned chicken

to the pan. Bring the liquid to a boil, then reduce to a medium heat and cover. Cook for around 15 to 20 minutes.

4. Uncover the pan and carefully remove the chicken. Mix in the drained rice and cooking liquid. Cook, uncovered, for 1 to 2 minutes over high heat. Replace the chicken on top of the rice. Decrease the flame, cover the pan, and keep cooking the rice and chicken for another 15 minutes, or until the rice is perfectly cooked. Turn the flame down but leave the pan covered and unattended for 10 minutes. Serve immediately.

Tasty sausages with peppers

Servings: 6

Nutrition: 250 Calories, 18g Fat, 11g Carbohydrates, 13g Protein, 780mg Sodium, 53mg Cholesterol

Ingredients:

- 1 pound grape or cherry tomatoes
- 3 garlic cloves, peeled and minced
- Few sprigs fresh thyme, about ⅛ ounce
- 1 tablespoon dried oregano
- 1 pound fully cooked chicken sausage links, mild or spicy
- 1 large red bell pepper, cored and cut into thin strips
- Black Pepper
- Extra virgin olive oil
- thin strips
- 1 large green pepper, cored and cut into thin strips
- 1 red onion, halved then sliced
- ½ teaspoon sweet paprika
- Kosher salt

Directions:

1. Start heating your oven to broil and place a rack about 6 inches from the heat source.
2. Score the sausage links numerous times without cutting all the way through.
3. In a mixing bowl, combine the bell peppers, onions, and tomatoes. Add garlic, fresh thyme, oregano, paprika, kosher salt, and black pepper to taste. Drizzle with extra virgin olive oil (a good sprinkle of 3 to 4 tablespoons or sufficient to cover the vegetables nicely) and toss to distribute the coating.
4. Place the vegetables on a large baking sheet in a single layer. Insert the sausage links, nestling them between the spread veggies.
5. Broil the baking sheet for 8 to 10 minutes, or until the vegetables are cooked and the sausage is beautifully browned.

Chicken with tomatoes

Servings: 4

Nutrition: 410 Calories, 14g Fat, 14g Carbohydrates, 50g Protein, 513mg Sodium, 145mg Cholesterol

Ingredients:

- 2 tablespoons extra virgin olive oil
- ½ cup dry white wine
- 1 large lemon, juiced
- ½ cup chicken broth
- 1 medium red onion, finely chopped
- 4 boneless, skinless chicken breasts
- 2 tablespoons minced garlic or garlic paste
- Handful of fresh parsley, stems removed, leaves chopped
- Crumbled feta cheese
- Kosher salt
- Black pepper
- 1 tablespoon dried oregano, divided
- 4 small tomatoes, diced, about 1 ½ cups
- ¼ cup sliced green olives

Directions:

1. Rinse the chicken breasts. Make three deep incisions in the chicken breast on each side.
2. Rub some garlic into the incisions you cut in the chicken on both sides. Sprinkle both sides of the chicken breasts with salt, pepper, and 12 teaspoon dried oregano.
3. Warm the olive oil in a big cast iron skillet over medium-high heat. Caramelize the chicken on all sides, then decrease the white wine by half. Combine the lemon juice and chicken broth in a mixing bowl. Reduce the temperature to medium and put the remaining 12 tablespoon oregano on top. Cover securely with a lid or foil.
4. Cook for 5 to 6 minutes on one side, then flip and cook for 5 to 6 minutes more, or until the core temperature of the chicken achieves 165°F.
5. Remove the cover and top with the chopped onions, tomatoes, and olives. Cook for another 3 minutes, covered. Finally, sprinkle with parsley and feta cheese. Enjoy!

Greek style grouper

Servings: 5

Nutrition: 185 Calories, 5g Fat, 7g Carbohydrates, 27g Protein, 130mg Sodium, 10mg Cholesterol

Ingredients:

- 1 tsp sweet paprika
- ½ tsp black pepper
- 4 large garlic cloves, minced
- Juice of 1 large lemon, more for later
- 1 ½ lb grouper fillet
- kosher salt
- 6 to 8 pitted kalamata olives, sliced
- Chopped fresh dill
- 1 tbsp dry oregano
- 1 to 1 ½ tsp ground cumin
- Extra virgin olive oil
- 6 to 8 oz cherry tomatoes, halved

Directions:

1. Preheat the oven to 400°F.
2. Pat the fish dry and sprinkle both sides with salt. Mix the spices (cumin, oregano, paprika, and black pepper) in a small bowl, then sprinkle the fish on both sides with the spice mixture.
3. Put the seasoned fish in a baking dish that has been lightly greased. Top with minced garlic, lemon juice, and a good sprinkle of extra virgin olive oil. Place the fish fillets on top of the cherry tomatoes and olives.
4. Bake for 12 to 13 minutes, or until the salmon is opaque and flakes readily with a fork.
5. Remove from the heat and sprinkle with fresh dill. Enjoy!

Baked fish with tomatoes and spices

Servings: 6

Nutrition: 310 Calories, 17g Fat, 13g Carbohydrates, 27g Protein, 147mg Sodium, 35mg Cholesterol

Ingredients:

- 1 tsp all-natural sweet Spanish paprika
- 1 tsp organic ground cumin
- ½ tsp cayenne pepper
- 1 ½ tbsp capers
- Salt and pepper
- ⅓ cup extra virgin olive oil
- 1 small red onion, finely chopped
- Zest of 1 lemon
- Fresh parsley or mint for garnish
- 2 large tomatoes, diced
- 10 garlic cloves, chopped
- 1 ½ lb white fish fillet such as cod fillet
- Juice of ½ lemon or more to your liking
- 1 ½ tsp organic ground coriander
- ⅓ cup golden raisins

Directions:

1. Make the sauce with the tomatoes and capers. Warm extra virgin olive oil in a small saucepan on a medium-high heat until shimmering but not smoking. Cook for 3 minutes, stirring frequently, until the onions begin to turn gold in color. Put raisins, tomatoes, spices, garlic, salt and pepper, capers. Bring to a boil, then reduce to a medium-low heat and leave to simmer for about 15 minutes.
2. Preheat the oven to 400°F.
3. Pat the fish dry and massage both sides with salt and pepper.
4. 12 of the cooked tomato sauce should be poured into the bottom of a 9 12" x 13" baking dish. Place the fish on top. Cover with the leftover tomato sauce after adding the lemon juice and zest.
5. Bake at 400°F for 15 to 18 minutes, or until fish is cooked through and flakes readily. Remove from the heat and top with fresh parsley or mint to taste.

Mediterranean Chicken Soup

Servings: 4

Nutrition: 170 Calories, 8g Carbohydrates, 26g Protein, 3g Fat, 180mg Sodium, 72mg Cholesterol

Ingredients:

- 2 carrots, peeled and thinly sliced into rounds
- 1 teaspoon coriander
- 1 teaspoon Aleppo Pepper
- ½ teaspoon ground ginger
- 1-pound boneless chicken breast
- 1 yellow onion, quartered
- ½ cup chopped fresh parsley
- Juice and zest of 2 lemons
- 4 large garlic cloves, divided (2 whole, 2 minced)
- Extra virgin olive oil
- 2 cups baby spinach
- ¼ cup chopped fresh dill
- ½ teaspoon turmeric

Directions:

1. Mix the chicken and 6 cups of water in a large saucepan. Add pepper and salt to taste. Add the onion and 2 garlic cloves, whole. Bring to a boil over moderate flame, then reduce to a low heat and cover for 15 to 20 minutes, or until the chicken is done.
2. When the chicken is done, take it from the saucepan and shred it with two forks. Pour the broth through a mesh filter into a large mixing basin. Remove the onion and garlic. Put aside the broth in its basin for the time being.
3. Bring the saucepan to the heat after carefully wiping it down. Cook over medium heat with a couple teaspoons extra virgin olive oil. Combine the chopped garlic, carrots, and spices in a small bowl.

4. Place the shredded chicken back to the skillet. To blend, everything together. Sprinkle with kosher salt to taste.
5. Bring the boiling broth to a boil, then reduce to a medium-low heat and partially cover. Cook for an another 15 to 20 minutes (the carrots should be soft and cooked through).
6. Incorporate the spinach, herbs, lemon juice, and zest. Arrange in serving dishes. Enjoy!

Greek chicken wings

Servings: 6

Nutrition: 403 Calories, 34g Fat, 3g Carbohydrates, 19g Protein, 82mg Sodium, 78mg Cholesterol

Ingredients:

- juice of 2 lemons
- 1 teaspoon sweet paprika
- 1 teaspoon coriander
- 1 large red onion, quartered
- 8 garlic cloves
- ½ teaspoon turmeric
- ½ teaspoon nutmeg
- ½ cup extra virgin olive oil
- 1 teaspoon cumin
- 1 teaspoon pepper
- 1 teaspoon coriander

Directions:

1. Mix the onion, garlic, olive oil, lemon juice, and spices in the bowl of a large food mixer fitted with a blade. Blend until everything is well incorporated into a rich sauce.
2. Put the chicken wings in a zip-top bag and sprinkle with Kosher salt. Drizzle the marinade over the top and seal the bag. Shake the bag to spread the sauce evenly.
3. Place the wings bag flat on a large plate or platter. Put it in the fridge for 2 to 4 hours, turning the bag over halfway.
4. Preheat the grill to 425°F and lightly oil the grates.
5. Shake off any excess marinade before placing the wings over direct heat.
6. Cook the wings for 15 to 20 minutes, flipping them over every 5 minutes, until well cooked through. Grill the lemons with the flesh side down.
7. Serve the wings with the grilled lemons right away. And then juice the lemons to your preference.

Chicken thighs with yogurt sauce

Servings: 8

Nutrition: 270 Calories, 7g Carbohydrates, 26g Protein, 15g Fat, 260mg Sodium, 108mg Cholesterol

Ingredients:

- 1 ¼ cup Greek yogurt
- 1 tablespoon Extra virgin olive oil
- 1 garlic clove, minced
- 1 cup fresh dill, stems removed, chopped
- Kosher salt
- ½ lemon or lime, juiced
- ½ teaspoon ground nutmeg
- ¼ teaspoon ground green cardamom
- Salt and pepper
- 10 garlic cloves minced
- ½ teaspoon paprika
- 1 red onion, halved and thinly sliced
- 2 lemons, juiced
- 5 tablespoon Extra virgin olive oil, divided
- 8 boneless skinless chicken thighs

Directions:

1. In a blender, mix the chopped garlic, cayenne pepper, dill, olive oil, yogurt, lemon juice. Process the blender until all of the ingredients are thoroughly combined and a smooth, thick sauce or dip forms. If necessary, add salt. Cover and place in the refrigerator in a small dish or container. In a small mixing dish, combine the spices, chopped garlic, and 3 tbsp olive oil. Next, massage the chicken tights with the garlic-spice mixture. Add the onions, lemon juice, and remaining olive oil to a big dish with sides (to keep the marinade). Stir the chicken with the onions for a few minutes to coat it in the olive oil and lemon juice.

2. Put it in the fridge the chicken for 2-4 hours if you have the time. Instead, grill the chicken thighs. Cover for 5 minutes, then flip the chicken and cover for another 3 to 5 minutes.
3. Let the grilled chicken to rest for 5 minutes before serving. When the chicken is done, the core temperature at the thickest area should be 165 degrees.
4. Serve alongside the dill Greek yogurt dip you made earlier!

Lemon flavoured salmon

Servings: 6

Nutrition: 390 Calories, 26g Fat, 12g Carbohydrates, 33g Protein, 7mg Sodium, 70mg Cholesterol

Ingredients:

- Kosher salt
- Extra virgin olive oil
- 2 lb salmon fillet
- ½ lemon, sliced into rounds
- Parsley for garnish
- 3 tbsp extra virgin olive oil
- 5 garlic cloves, chopped
- Zest of 1 large lemon
- Juice of 2 lemons
- 1 tsp sweet paprika
- ½ tsp black pepper
- 2 tsp dry oregano

Directions:

1. Preheat the oven to 375°F.
2. Prepare the garlic-lemon sauce. Combine the lemon juice, lemon zest, extra virgin olive oil, garlic, oregano, paprika, and black pepper in a small bowl. Mix the sauce well.
3. Take a big sheet pan lined with foil (should be big enough to fold over salmon). Drizzle the foil with extra virgin olive oil on top.
4. Pat salmon dry and sprinkle both sides liberally with kosher salt. Put it on the foil-lined baking sheet. Serve with lemon garlic sauce on top.

Salmon with balsamic glaze

Servings: 8

Nutrition: 210 Calories, 8g Fat, 8g Carbohydrates, 25g Protein, 325mg Sodium, 60mg Cholesterol

Ingredients:

- 4 garlic cloves, minced
- ½ tsp cayenne pepper
- ½ tsp Aleppo pepper
- 1 cup balsamic vinegar
- ¼ cup quality dark honey
- 3 tbsp Dijon mustard
- 2 tbsp extra virgin olive oil
- Salt and black pepper
- ⅓ cup chopped fresh parsley leaves
- 3 lb Salmon fillet, no skin
- ⅓ cup chopped fresh dill

Directions:

1. Preheat the oven to 425°F.
2. Mix balsamic vinegar and honey in a small skillet. Bring to a boil over moderate flame before lowering to a simmer. Cook for around 15 minutes. Remove from the fire and set aside for 5 minutes to cool.
3. Add the garlic, spices, mustard, and olive oil to the balsamic marinade. Stir until everything is well blended.
4. Using parchment paper, line a large baking sheet.
5. Toss the salmon on both sides with salt and black pepper. Coat one side of the salmon with the balsamic glaze, then place it, glazed side down, on the already-prepared baking sheet. Brush the top liberally with the balsamic glaze. Save a small amount of the glaze aside for the end.
6. Put the salmon in the oven and bake until it flakes easily. The baking time for your salmon will be decided by the thickness of the thickest region of the salmon fillet. Roast for 8 to 10 minutes per inch of thickness. It could take between 15 and 18 minutes.

7. Remove from oven and brush the remaining glaze over the top. Garnish with fresh chopped herbs. Enjoy!

Salmon with feta and veggies

Servings: 4

Nutrition: 380 Calories, 19g Fat, 12g Carbohydrates, 42g Protein, 625mg Sodium, 125mg Cholesterol

Ingredients:

- 1 bell pepper, any color, cored and sliced into thin sticks
- 5 ounces baby bella mushrooms, trimmed and halved
- 4 to 5 large garlic cloves, peeled
- 5 to 6 ounces feta cheese block, cut into large chunks
- 2 teaspoon dried oregano
- 1 teaspoon sumac
- 4 6-ounce portions salmon fillet
- 1 to 2 large lemons, halved, for serving
- 1 teaspoon cumin
- 1 cup cherry tomatoes
- Kosher salt and black pepper
- Extra virgin olive oil
- 6 to 7 sprigs of fresh thyme

Directions:

1. Preheat the oven to 425°F and place a rack in the center.
2. Mix the oregano, sumac, and cumin in a small basin.
3. Place the tomatoes, mushrooms, bell peppers, and 4 to 5 entire garlic cloves in a baking tray or sheet pan. Place the feta slices in between. Sprinkle with 1 ½ tablespoons of the spice combination and a big sprinkling of kosher salt and black pepper. Add a couple fresh thyme sprigs. Pour 1 to 2 tablespoons olive oil over the top.
4. Put the sheet pan on the center rack of the preheated oven. Bake for 5 to 10 minutes, or until the vegetables are tender.
5. Next, pat the fish dry and brush both sides with kosher salt, black pepper and the spice mixture.
6. Remove the sheet pan from the oven and combine the fish, vegetables, and feta.
7. Place the sheet pan to the center rack of the preheated oven and wrap it in foil. Sauté for 10 minutes, or until the fish is warmed through and readily flakes. Take the fish from the oven and quickly drizzle lemon juice over it.

Beef ribs in wine with potatoes

Servings: 6

Nutrition: 760 Calories, 40g Fat, 50g Carbohydrates, 50g Protein, 1250mg Sodium, 77mg Cholesterol

Directions:

1. The oven must be preheated at 300 degrees F.
2. In a mixing bowl, add 12 teaspoon seasoned salt, 1 teaspoon pepper, paprika, and ground cardamom. Season the short ribs liberally on all sides.
3. In a large braising pot, heat 2 tbsp of vegetable oil. Over medium-high heat, caramelize the short ribs on both sides. Set aside after removing from the saucepan.
4. Increase the heat to medium and sauté the potatoes, celery, and red onion for about 10 minutes, tossing periodically. Garnish the vegetables with seasoned salt and black pepper to taste. Remove from the saucepan and leave aside for a few minutes.

Ingredients:

- Vegetable oil
- 2-3 large russet potatoes, peeled, washed, cut into 2-inch pieces
- 3 celery stalks roughly chopped
- 1 large red onion roughly chopped
- 5 large garlic cloves, lightly crushed
- Seasoned salt
- Black pepper
- 1 cup red wine
- 4-5 cups low-sodium beef broth
- 1 tsp ground green cardamom
- 3 lb bone-in beef short ribs; ask the butcher to trim fat and cut short ribs into smaller 3-inch pieces
- 2 tsp paprika
- 1 tbsp all-purpose flour
- 1 15-oz can diced tomatoes
- 5 fresh sage leaves
- 2 bay leaves

5. Now in the same saucepan, place baby leaves, sage, garlic and diced tomatoes. Sauté for 5-7 minutes, or until the tomato has turned a rusty red. Then, to coat the tomatoes, whisk in the flour.
6. Increase the heat to high and add the red wine and broth. Cook for 7 minutes on high heat until the liquid is somewhat reduced. To taste, add a dash of seasoned salt.
7. Return the meat and sautéed vegetables to the saucepan and simmer for another 5-7 minutes on medium-high, uncovered.
8. Cover the pot and bake for two hours, or until the short ribs are fork-tender, at 300°F. Garnish with your favorite crusty bread in bowls!

Beef stew with green beans

Servings: 4

Nutrition: 385 Calories, 23g Fat, 20g Carbohydrates, 32g Protein, 210mg Sodium, 98mg Cholesterol

Ingredients:

- 3 garlic cloves, chopped
- 3 Roma tomatoes, chopped
- 3 tbsp tomato paste
- 1 tsp paprika
- ½ tsp ground cinnamon
- 1 lb beef stew meat cut into 1-inch cubes
- Salt and Pepper
- 3 tbsp toasted pine nuts
- Handful parsley leaves for garnish, stems removed
- 1 tbsp all-purpose flour
- Olive oil
- 1 bay leaf
- 1 lb frozen cut green beans
- 1 small yellow onion, chopped
- 2 ½ cups water

Directions:

1. Sprinkle the beef with salt and pepper and lightly coat with all-purpose flour on all sides.
2. 1 tablespoon olive oil, heated in a large cooking pot. Brown the beef all over. Take the meat from the pot and set it aside for a moment.
3. Mix the diced onion and garlic in the hot saucepan for a few seconds on medium-high heat. Combine the tomatoes and tomato paste in a mixing bowl. Add paprika, cinnamon, coriander, salt, and pepper to taste. Cook for 3 minutes on medium-high.
4. Return the steak to the pot, along with the water and bay leaf.
5. Bring everything to a boil for 5 minutes, then reduce to a low heat for 12 hours.
6. Uncover and mix in the frozen green beans, along with a pinch of salt. Add a bit more water if necessary. Mix once more and continue to cook on low for 45 minutes. Remove the bay leaf from the pot and turn off the heat.
7. Move the beef stew to serving bowls and serve with rice or your favorite bread. Sprinkle with toasted pine nuts and fresh parsley, if desired. Enjoy!

Italian fish soup

Servings: 6

Nutrition: 320 Calories, 12g Fat, 20g Carbohydrates, 32g Protein, 800mg Sodium, 88 mg Cholesterol

Ingredients:

- ½ tsp dried thyme
- Pinch red pepper flakes
- ¾ cup dry white wine
- 1 28-oz can whole peeled plum tomatoes, juice separated and reserved
- 3 cups low-sodium vegetable broth
- extra virgin olive oil
- 1 large yellow onion, chopped
- 3 tbsp toasted pine nuts, optional
- Crusty Italian bread for serving
- 2 celery ribs, chopped
- Salt and pepper
- 4 large garlic cloves, minced
- 2 tbsp capers, rinsed
- 2 lb skinless sea bass fillet, about 1 ½-inch thick, cut into large cubes
- ½ cup chopped fresh parsley leaves, stems removed

Directions:

1. In a 5-quart cast iron, heat 1 tablespoon olive oil over medium high heat. Add the onions, celery, and a pinch of salt and pepper (12 tsp each). Cook, stirring occasionally, until caramelized (about 4 minutes). Cook until the thyme, red pepper flakes, and garlic are fragrant (about 30 more seconds).
2. Mix in the white wine and tomato juice from the can. Bring to a simmer and boil until the liquid has been reduced by about 12 percent. Combine the tomatoes, vegetable broth, raisins, and capers in a mixing bowl. Sauté for 15-20 minutes over medium heat, or until the flavors meld.
3. Pat the fish dry and add pepper and salt to taste. Place the fish pieces in the cooking liquid and gently swirl everything together so that the fish pieces are well covered in the cooking liquid. Bring to a simmer and continue to boil for 5 minutes. Turn off the heat and cover the cast iron. Let the fish to finish cooking for another 4-5 minutes off the heat. While gently pulling apart the fish with a paring knife, it should be flaky. Lastly, incorporate the parsley.
4. Spoon the hot fish stew into two bowls and garnish with toasted pine nuts, if desired. End up serving with crusty bread of your choice!

Greek fish fillet

Servings: 6

Nutrition: 177 Calories, 3g Fat, 11g Carbohydrates, 29g Protein, 187mg Sodium, 54mg Cholesterol

Ingredients:

- 1 large yellow onion (or sweet onion), chopped
- Extra virgin olive oil
- 8 garlic cloves, chopped
- 2 jalapeno peppers, chopped
- 5 medium ripe tomatoes, diced or chopped
- 2 tsp ground coriander
- 2 tsp sumac
- ½ cup chopped fresh parsley for garnish
- 1 tbsp chopped fresh mint leaves for garnish
- 1 ½ tsp ground cumin
- 1 tsp dry dill weed
- 1 tsp turmeric
- ½ cup water
- salt and pepper
- 2 lb cod fillet cut into large 4 to 6-ounce pieces

Directions:

1. To prepare the spice mix, put the coriander, sumac, cumin, dill, and turmeric in a mixing bowl. Put away until required.
2. Warm 2 tablespoon olive oil, heated in a big, deep pan (with a lid). Cook the onions for 2 minutes before adding the garlic and jalapeño. Sauté for another 2 minutes over medium-high, stirring frequently, until aromatic and golden in color.
3. Then add the tomatoes and 12 of the spice mixture. Combine the lime juice, salt and pepper, water, lime juice and tomato paste in a mixing bowl. To blend, stir

everything together. Bring to a boil, then reduce to a medium-low heat. Cook the tomato mixture, covered, for 10 minutes more, stirring periodically.
4. Next, sprinkle the fish fillets liberally with salt and pepper and sprinkle both sides with the leftover 12 teaspoon spice mixture.
5. Carefully fold the fish fillets into the tomato mixture, nestling them nicely. Cook for a few minutes on medium-high, then reduce to medium. Cook for another 10-15 minutes, or until the salmon is cooked completely (it should be flaky).
6. Remove from the heat and sprinkle with fresh parsley and mint leaves. Serve immediately with your favorite crusty bread in bowls.

Super tasty shrimps with bell peppers

Servings: 4

Nutrition: 285 Calories, 3g Fat, 10g Carbohydrates, 31g Protein, 1260mg Sodium, 360mg Cholesterol

Ingredients:
- ¼ teaspoon cayenne
- ¼ teaspoon sugar
- 1 tablespoon butter
- 3 tablespoon Extra virgin olive oil
- ½ red onion, thinly sliced
- 1 ¼ lb large shrimp or prawns, peeled and deveined
- 1 tablespoon all-purpose flour
- 2 tablespoon fresh lemon juice
- ⅓ cup chopped parsley leaves
- ½ teaspoon each salt and pepper
- ½ teaspoon ground coriander
- ⅓ cup chicken or vegetable broth
- 2 tablespoon dry white wine
- 1 to 2 teaspoons smoked paprika
- 4 garlic cloves, chopped
- ½ green bell pepper and ½ yellow bell pepper, cored and sliced
- 1 cup canned diced tomato

Directions:

1. Put the shrimp in a large mixing dish and pat dry. Combine the flour, smoked paprika, salt and pepper, coriander, cayenne pepper, and sugar in a mixing bowl. Stir the shrimp until evenly coated.
2. Melt the butter and olive oil in a big cast iron skillet over medium heat. Stir in the shallots and garlic. Sauté, stirring frequently, for 2-3 minutes, or until aromatic. Cook for another 4 minutes, stirring regularly, after adding the bell peppers.
3. Add the shrimp now. Sauté for 1–2 minutes before adding the diced tomatoes, broth, white wine, and lemon juice. Sauté for a few minutes longer, or until the shrimp turn brilliant orange.
4. Lastly, fold in the fresh parsley and enjoy!

Middle Eastern lamb meatballs with onions

Servings: 5

Nutrition: 113 Calories, 3g Carbohydrates, 6g Protein, 9g Fat, 32mg Sodium, 28mg Cholesterol

Ingredients:

- 1 ½ pounds ground lamb
- ⅓ cup breadcrumbs
- ½ bunch fresh parsley, leaves chopped
- 1 egg
- 3 tablespoons extra virgin olive oil
- 3 medium yellow onions, sliced into ¼-inch rings
- ¼ teaspoon ground cardamom
- Black pepper
- 1 small yellow onion, grated
- Kosher salt
- 2 garlic cloves, minced

Directions:

1. Set the oven temperature to 425 degrees Fahrenheit.
2. Warm the olive oil in a big oven-safe skillet over medium-high heat. When it shimmers. Sprinkle with a generous teaspoon of salt and add the chopped onion rings. Simmer, stirring periodically, for 20-30 minutes, or until the onions have softened completely and turned a deep golden brown.
3. In a big bowl, mix the grated onion, lamb, breadcrumbs, parsley, egg, garlic, and cardamom while the onions are frying. Mix in a generous teaspoon of kosher salt and black pepper. Form meatballs with handfuls of the meat mixture (approximately 2 tablespoons each). You should have roughly 18-20 meatballs.
4. Remove from the heat and gradually mix in 1 cup of water when the onions are done. The water should quickly become brown. Place the lamb meatballs in the onion sauce and spoon some of the onions over.
5. Bake the pan on the center rack for 25 to 30 minutes, or until the meatballs are cooked completely and no longer pink in the centre. Enjoy.

Spanish-style chicken

Servings: 6

Nutrition: 460 Calories, 20g Carbohydrates, 25g Protein, 30g Fat, 470mg Sodium, 95mg Cholesterol

Ingredients:

- ½ cup pitted Spanish green olives
- ¼ cup capers, with a little bit of juice
- ¼ cup red wine vinegar
- ¼ cup extra virgin olive oil
- 1 whole chicken, cut up
- 3 bay leaves
- ½ cup white wine
- ¼ cup brown sugar
- 1 head garlic, peeled
- ½ cup pitted prunes
- 2 tablespoons dried oregano
- Kosher salt
- pepper

Directions:

1. Cut the backbone out of a whole chicken with sharp kitchen scissors. Next, on above, press down to split the remaining bones. Remove the legs and thighs first, followed by the wings and tips.
2. Mix bay leaves, garlic cloves, prunes, olives, capers, red wine vinegar, olive oil, dried oregano, salt, and pepper in a large mixing basin. Mix it everything together before adding the chicken. Squish it around. Lift the skin slightly to allow the marinade to adhere to the chicken's flesh as well.
3. Put the bowl in the refrigerator overnight, covered, otherwise, if you don't have time, rest it rest for 30 minutes.
4. Set the oven temperature to 350°F. Place the chicken and marinade, including the prunes, olives, and other ingredients, in a large oven-safe pan and distribute it out uniformly so the chicken pieces do

not stand on top of each other. Fill the baking dish halfway with wine. Pour brown sugar over the top of the chicken and bake for 50 to 60 minutes. While the chicken cooks, baste it with the pan juices a few times.

5. When the core temperature of the chicken hits 165°F and the skin turns golden brown, it is done. Place the chicken on a big plate and garnish with the olives, prunes and capers.
6. Bring the roasting pan juices to a boil over medium high heat and reduce until you have about 12 cups of sauce. Pour the sauce over the chicken after straining it into a bowl. Serve and have fun!

Salad dishes

Fresh fruit salad

Servings: 6

Nutrition: 230 Calories, 44g Carbohydrates, 3g Protein, 7g Fat, 6mg Sodium, 3mg Cholesterol

Ingredients:
- Juice of 2 large limes
- ¼ cup orange juice
- 2 to 3 tablespoons honey, warmed
- 3 Clementine oranges, peeled and segmented
- 3 kiwis, peeled and thinly sliced into rounds
- ½ cup chopped walnuts
- 6 to 10 fresh mint leaves, chopped
- 2 large apples, cored and thinly sliced
- 2 Bosc pears, cored and thinly sliced
- 1 cup pomegranate arils

Directions:

1. In a large mixing basin, whisk together the first three ingredients: honey, lime juice, and orange juice.
2. Mix in all of the fruit and walnuts. If used, sprinkle with mint. Mix everything together until everything is fully integrated. Serve!

Greek-style tuna salad

Servings: 6

Nutrition: 190 Calories, 6g Carbohydrates, 12g Protein, 15g Fat, 370mg Sodium, 20mg Cholesterol

Ingredients:

- 1 ½ limes, juice of
- ⅓ cup extra virgin olive oil
- 2 ½ teaspoon good quality Dijon mustard
- Zest of 1 lime
- ½ teaspoon sumac
- Pinch of kosher salt and black pepper
- 4-5 radishes, stems removed, chopped
- 3 green onions, both white and green parts, chopped
- ½ medium red onion, finely chopped
- 1 bunch parsley, stems removed, chopped (about 1 cup chopped fresh parsley)
- 10-15 fresh mint leaves, stems removed, finely chopped (about ½ cup chopped fresh mint)
- 3 cans tuna, 5 ounces each
- 2 ½ celery stalks, chopped
- ½ cup cup pitted Kalamata olives, halved
- ½ English cucumber, chopped

Directions:

1. To prepare the zesty mustard vinaigrette, mix together the Dijon mustard, lime zest, and lime juice in a mixing bowl. Stir in the olive oil, sumac, salt and pepper, until completely combined. Put aside for a moment.
2. To create the tuna salad, mix the tuna with the sliced veggies, Kalamata olives, chopped fresh parsley, and mint leaves in a big salad bowl. Using a wooden spoon, gently combine the ingredients.
3. Toss the tuna salad with the dressing. Stir one more to ensure that the tuna salad is completely mixed with the dressing. Put it in the fridge for 30 minutes before serving, covered. When ready to serve, lightly toss the salad to refresh it.

Mediterranean veggies salad

Servings: 8

Nutrition: 210 Calories, 28g Carbohydrates, 10g Protein, 8g Fat, 480mg Sodium, 5mh Cholesterol

Ingredients:

- 1 red bell pepper, cored and chopped
- ½ English cucumber, diced
- 1 cup chopped red onions
- 1 ½ tablespoon capers, drained
- 1 15 oz can kidney beans, drained and rinsed
- 1 15- oz can cannellini beans, drained and rinsed
- 10-15 fresh mint leaves, chopped
- 10-15 fresh basil leaves, chopped
- 1 15- oz can garbanzo beans (chickpeas), drained and rinsed
- 1 green bell pepper, cored and chopped
- 1 cup chopped fresh parsley
- 2 tablespoon lemon juice
- 1 teaspoon sugar
- 1-2 garlic cloves minced
- ½ tablespoon Dijon mustard
- ¼ cup extra virgin olive oil
- Salt and black pepper

Directions:

1. Mix the beans, chopped peppers, onions, capers, and fresh herbs in a large mixing basin. With a wooden spoon, combine the ingredients.
2. To make the vinaigrette, combine the last 6 ingredients in a small bowl. To blend, whisk vigorously.
3. Pour the vinaigrette over the salad. To coat, toss with a fork.
4. Cover and chill for a few minutes before serving to allow the beans to soak up the vinaigrette tastes. Before serving, give the salad another short spin.

Salad with watermelon and feta

Servings: 6

Nutrition: 52 Calories, 7g Carbohydrates, 3g Protein, 2g Fat, 113 mg Sodium, 7mg Cholesterol

Ingredients:

- 2 tablespoon lime juice
- 1 to 2 tablespoon quality extra virgin olive oil
- 2 tablespoon honey
- pinch of salt
- 1 cucumber, cubed (about 2 cupfuls of cubed cucumbers)
- 15 fresh mint leaves chopped
- ½ watermelon peeled, cut into cubes
- 15 fresh basil leaves chopped
- ½ cup crumbled feta cheese

Directions:

1. In a small mixing bowl, combine the honey, lime juice, olive oil, and pinch of salt.
2. Then mix the watermelon, cucumbers, and fresh herbs in a large mixing basin or serving dish with sides.
3. Stir the watermelon salad with the dressing until well combined. Serve with the feta cheese on top!

Tomato salad with feta

Servings: 6

Nutrition: 130 Calories, 5g Carbohydrates, 2g Protein, 10g Fat, 55mg Sodium, 5mg Cholesterol

Ingredients:

- 1 cup packed chopped fresh dill, chopped
- 2 ½ teaspoon ground sumac
- Kosher salt
- Black pepper
- 6 to 7 medium ripe tomatoes, sliced into wedges
- 1 medium red onion, halved, then thinly sliced
- ⅓ cup extra virgin olive oil
- Feta cheese, to your liking
- 3 garlic cloves, minced
- 1 cup packed chopped fresh parsley leaves, chopped
- 1 lemon, juice of
- 2 teaspoon white wine vinegar

Directions:

1. Combine the tomatoes, onions, fresh herbs, and garlic in a large salad or mixing dish.
2. Add sumac, kosher salt, and freshly ground pepper to taste. Combine the lemon juice, white wine vinegar, and extra virgin olive oil in a mixing bowl. To mix, toss everything together. Season with salt and pepper to taste.
3. Place on a serving dish or bowl. Large chunks of high-quality feta cheese go on top. Enjoy!

Orange and pomegranate salad

Servings: 6

Nutrition: 150 Calories, 3g Fat, 33g Carbohydrates, 3g Protein, 200mg Sodium, 7mg Cholesterol

Ingredients:

- 6 Navel oranges, peeled, sliced into rounds
- Pinch kosher salt
- 1 ½ oz thinly sliced red onions (about 1 cup)
- 25 fresh mint leaves, chopped
- pinch ground cinnamon
- Seeds (arils) of 1 pomegranate
- Pinch sweet paprika
- 1 tbsp extra virgin olive oil
- 1 tbsp honey
- 1 lime, juice

Directions:

1. Prepare the dressing. Combine the lime juice, olive oil, honey, and orange blossom water in a small mixing basin. Set aside.
2. Put the chopped onions in a dish of ice-cold water to soak. Let for 5-10 minutes before removing the onions from the water and properly drying them.
3. Assemble a serving dish. Place half of the minced mint leaves on the tray, followed by the orange slices and onions. Add a bit of salt, sweet paprika, and cinnamon to taste. Now sprinkle with the pomegranate seeds.
4. Dress the orange pomegranate salad with the dressing.
5. Lastly, garnish with the leftover fresh mint leaves.

Leave aside for about 5 minutes before serving.

Berry salad with burrata and arugula

Servings: 4

Nutrition: 240 Calories, 18g Carbohydrates, 8g Protein, 5g Fat, 20mg Cholesterol, 277mg Sodium

Ingredients:

- 6 oz fresh blackberries
- 6 oz fresh raspberries
- 6 oz baby arugula
- 1 small shallot halved and sliced
- 6 oz fresh strawberries
- 4 oz Burrata cheese
- 1 large lemon, juice
- kosher salt and black pepper
- 3 tablespoon extra virgin olive oil

Directions:

1. Prepare the dressing. In a small bowl, combine the extra virgin olive oil, lemon juice, salt, and pepper. To blend, whisk everything together.
2. Combine the arugula, shallots, and berries in a large mixing bowl (all three berry varieties). Toss the salad with the dressing.
3. Place the berry salad on a serving plate and top with the burrata cheese. Enjoy!

Nutritious salad with avocado

Servings: 4

Nutrition: 215 Calories, 20g Fat, 13g Carbohydrates, 3g Protein, 16mg Sodium, 3mg Cholesterol

Ingredients:

- ½ English cucumber, halved lengthwise, then sliced
- 1 shallot, sliced
- 5 oz baby arugula
- 1 to 2 vine ripe tomatoes, cut into wedges
- 1 avocado, pitted and sliced
- 1 to 2 garlic cloves, minced
- 1 tsp dry oregano
- ¼ cup extra virgin olive oil
- Zest and juice of 1 large lemon
- Kosher salt
- Black pepper

Directions:

1. Combine the olive oil, lemon zest and juice, garlic, oregano, kosher salt, and pepper in a large mixing basin. To blend, whisk everything together.
2. Add tomatoes, cucumbers, shallots, arugula, and sliced avocado. To mix, toss everything together. Season with salt and pepper to taste.
3. Serve the salad on a serving plate. Serve right away.

Salad with brussels sprouts and dried fruit

Servings: 6

Nutrition: 250 Calories, 24g Carbohydrates, 6g Protein, 17g Fat, 102mg Sodium, 5mg Cholesterol

Ingredients:

- 2 shallots, peeled and thinly sliced
- 1 large apple, halved and thinly sliced
- Handful crumbled feta cheese
- 1 pound Brussels sprouts
- 6 ounces baby arugula
- Handful walnut hearts
- Handful raisins and/or dried cranberries
- 1 red bell pepper, cored and sliced into thin sticks
- 1 tablespoon honey, more to your liking
- 1 garlic clove, minced
- ⅓ cup extra virgin olive oil
- 1 large lemon, juice
- Kosher salt
- Black pepper
- 1 to 2 tablespoons apple cider vinegar

Directions:

1. Mix together the olive oil, lemon juice, apple cider, honey, garlic, salt, pepper, and sumac in a small bowl. Put aside for the time being. To begin, cut the stem and remove any damaged leaves. Clean and pat dry the brussels sprouts. You may now shave them with a blender fitted with a slicing attachment. Pulse the Brussels sprouts until thinly cut.
2. Rinse and thoroughly drain shredded Brussels sprouts.
3. In a large mixing basin, combine the shaved brussels sprouts. Combine the baby arugula, bell peppers, shallots, and apple pieces in a mixing bowl. Mix the dressing with a fork before pouring it over the salad. Combine the feta cheese, walnut hearts, raisins, and cranberries in a mixing bowl. Gently toss the salad once more. Enjoy!

Mediterranean panzanella salad

Servings: 6

Nutrition: 83 Calories, 7g Carbohydrates, 5g Protein, 4g Fat, 22mg Sodium, 3mg Cholesterol

Ingredients:

- ¼ cup red wine vinegar
- 2 garlic cloves minced
- ½ teaspoon Dijon mustard
- 1 teaspoon fresh thyme optional
- 5 oz or ½ loaf of a rustic Italian bread cut into 1-inch cubes
- Extra virgin olive oil
- ½ cup packed fresh basil torn
- 4 oz fresh baby mozzarella
- Kosher salt
- 2 ¼ lb ripe tomatoes, cut into cubes
- Black pepper
- 2 Small shallots peeled and thinly sliced

Directions:

1. Preheat the oven to 400°F.
2. Mix bread cubes with a liberal sprinkle of extra virgin olive oil and a pinch of kosher salt in a large mixing dish. Mix to coat the bread completely. Place the bread cubes on a baking sheet and bake for about 10 minutes, or until browned. The edges should crisp up, while the bread develops some colour and crunchy but remains a little mushy.
3. Set a big colander over the mixing bowl. Put the tomatoes in a colander and season with kosher salt. Toss your hand briefly. Let the tomatoes to release their juices in the pan for a few minutes.
4. In a large mixing basin, combine the shaved brussels sprouts. Combine the baby arugula, bell peppers, shallots, and apple pieces in a mixing bowl. Mix the

dressing with a fork before pouring it over the salad. Combine the feta cheese, walnut hearts, raisins, and cranberries in a mixing bowl. Gently toss the salad once more. Enjoy!

Mix of brussels sprouts and mushrooms

Servings: 6

Nutrition: 180 Calories, 10g Fat, 23g Carbohydrates, 5g Protein, 420mg Sodium, 7mg Cholesterol

Ingredients:

- 1 large red onion, halved and sliced
- 1 tsp garlic powder
- ½ tsp cardamom
- ½ tsp cinnamon
- extra virgin olive oil
- 12 oz baby portabello mushrooms, cleaned, trimmed and sliced
- ½ cup dried cranberries
- ⅓ cup roughly chopped hazelnuts
- Salt
- 1.5 lb Brussels sprouts, trimmed and halved
- 1 to 2 teaspoon fresh lemon juice

Directions:

1. Put 1 tablespoon extra-virgin olive oil, heated in a big cast iron skillet on medium high until shimmering but not smoking. Add the mushrooms. Sauté, stirring occasionally, until browned (about 5 minutes). Add a pinch of salt and set the mushrooms aside till later.
2. Return the skillet to the stovetop. Warm 14 cup extra virgin olive oil on medium high. Mix in the Brussels sprouts and onions. Garlic powder, cardamom, and cinnamon, to taste. Sauté until the sprouts are crunchy and golden brown, turning periodically. Onions will caramelize as they cook down. Season liberally with salt.
3. Return the mushrooms to the pan to heat through.
4. Turn off the heat. Toss in the lemon juice. Season with salt and pepper to taste. Top with a sprinkle of extra virgin olive oil. Combine the cranberries and hazelnuts in a mixing bowl.
5. Place on a serving plate. Enjoy!

Asparagus salad with tomatoes

Servings: 6

Nutrition: 120 Calories, 7g Carbohydrates, 3g Protein, 9g Fat, 7mg Sodium, 2mg Cholesterol

Ingredients:

- Extra virgin olive oil
- 3 cups grape tomatoes halved
- 1 ½ pound asparagus, hard end trimmed
- Salt
- 15 large basil leaves, torn
- Feta
- ¼ cup extra virgin olive oil
- 1 garlic clove, minced
- ¼ cup sherry reserve vinegar or white wine vinegar
- salt and pepper

Directions:

1. Prepare the oven for 400 degrees Fahrenheit.
2. Arrange the asparagus stalks on a large baking sheet that has been lightly greased. Season with salt. Pour with extra virgin olive oil, mix to cover, and place asparagus in a single layer. Roast for 15 to 20 minutes, or until tender, in a preheated oven. Take from the heat and set aside to cool somewhat.
3. Mix together the vinegar, extra virgin olive oil, garlic, sumac, salt, and pepper to prepare the vinaigrette.
4. Place the grape tomatoes and feta in a mixing dish and mix with the sherry vinaigrette.
5. Place the roasted asparagus on a dish and serve with the tomato and cheese mixture. Then, stir in the basil leaves. Enjoy.

Super tasty cherry tomatoes salad

Servings: 6

Nutrition: 55 Calories, 6g Carbohydrates, 2g Protein, 3g Fat, 466mg Sodium, 3mg Cholesterol

Ingredients:

- ¼ cup chopped parsley
- 2 garlic cloves, minced
- Kosher salt and black pepper
- 4 cups cherry tomatoes, halved
- 1 cup pitted olives, chopped
- Zest and juice of 1 lime
- Extra virgin olive oil
- 1 teaspoon red pepper flakes
- 2 to 3 slices sourdough bread, cut into triangles

Directions:

1. Mix the tomatoes, olives, parsley, and garlic in a large mixing basin. Season with kosher salt, black pepper, and red pepper flakes to taste.
2. Mix in the lime juice and zest, as well as a generous pour of extra virgin olive oil. To mix, toss everything together.
3. Let 10 to 15 minutes for the tomatoes to release their juices before serving.
4. Next, serving with bread, lightly cook the sourdough triangles in olive oil. Heat 2 to 3 tablespoons extra virgin olive oil in a large saucepan on a low heat until slightly bubbling. Fry the bread triangles for a minute or two, or until crunchy and golden brown on both sides.
5. To remove extra oil from the bread, place it on a big platter lined with paper towels. Enjoy with the cherry tomato salad.

Tomato salad with burrata and prosciutto

Servings: 6

Nutrition: 295 Calories, 27g Carbohydrates, 14g Protein, 7g Fat, 528mg Sodium, 36mg Cholesterol

Ingredients:

- 1 cup grape or cherry tomatoes, halved
- 1 Jalapeno, seeded and minced
- 3 ounces sun-dried tomatoes, chopped
- ⅓ cup olives
- 8 ounces crusty Italian-style bread, like ciabatta
- Extra virgin olive oil
- Kosher salt and black pepper
- Red pepper flakes
- 8 ounces burrata cheese
- 3 ounces prosciutto
- 2 teaspoons capers
- Basil leaves, handful, torn

Directions:

1. Cut the bread into pieces and place them on a sheet pan, crusty side down. Sprinkle with extra virgin olive oil, spreading it over the soft side of the bread. Broil for a few minutes, watching carefully for the bread to brown.
2. Place the toasted bread on a large plate. Top with the other ingredients after adding the burrata, prosciutto, and tomatoes.
3. Garnish with kosher salt and black pepper, especially on the tomatoes and burrata, and a pinch of red pepper flakes if you don't mind the heat. Drizzle with olive oil and serve.

Gourmet Greek Chicken Salad

Servings: 4

Nutrition: 335 Calories, 12g Carbohydrates, 44g Protein, 2g Fat, 225mg Sodium, 112mg Cholesterol

Ingredients:

- 3 garlic cloves minced
- Kosher salt generous pinch to taste
- Black pepper generous pinch to taste
- 1 tablespoon oregano
- 1 cup Greek yogurt
- Juice of 1 large lemon
- 1 teaspoon ground coriander
- 1.5 lb Chicken tenders
- 2 tablespoon extra-virgin olive oil more for later
- 2 tablespoon red wine vinegar
- 1 teaspoon sweet paprika
- 1 teaspoon ground cumin
- 1 bell pepper any color, cored and chopped
- 1 English cucumber sliced into rounds, diced
- 2 shallots, thinly sliced
- 8 oz hearts of Romaine lettuce, chopped
- 10 oz cherry or grape tomatoes
- Pitted Kalamata olives, to your liking
- Quality Greek feta blocks

Directions:

1. Mix the yogurt, olive oil, lemon juice, vinegar, garlic, salt, and spices in a big bowl. Stir in the chicken tenders to ensure they are well covered with the marinade. Put it in the fridge for 30 minutes, covered.
2. Mix the lettuce, cherry tomatoes, bell pepper, cucumber slices, shallots, and kalamata olives in a large mixing basin. To taste, add feta cheese.
3. In a fry pan, warm 1 tablespoon extra virgin olive oil over medium high heat until shimmering. Add the chicken tenders to the pan, shaking off any leftover marinade before adding the chicken. Sauté for 5 minutes on one side, undisturbed, until golden. Turn the chicken over with a pair of tongs and cook for another 5 minutes, or until done.
4. Put together the grilled chicken salad. Place the salad in serving bowls and top with the cooked chicken. Serve right away.

Appetizers

Potato pancakes

Servings: 8

Nutrition: 150 Calories, 25g Carbohydrates, 5g Protein, 3g Fat, 173mg Sodium, 29mg Cholesterol

Ingredients:

- ¼ cup all-purpose flour
- 3 scallions, both white and green parts, chopped
- Extra Virgin Olive Oil for pan frying
- 3 cups chilled mashed potatoes, already cooked and stored in the fridge
- 1 egg
- ⅓ to ½ cup plain breadcrumbs
- ½ cup feta cheese, crumbled
- ¼ cup chopped fresh parsley

Directions:

1. Mix the mashed potatoes, feta, all-purpose flour, scallions, and parsley in a large mixing basin. Crack the egg and place it in the mixing bowl. Stir everything together with a wooden spoon until everything is properly combined. Place the breadcrumbs on a plate adjacent to the bowl containing the mashed potato mixture. Scoop a part of the mashed potato mixture to fill a measuring cup (14 cup or 13 cup, according to the dimensions of the patties you want). Make a ball with your hands, then lightly flatten into a 12-inch-thick patty. Dip the patty in breadcrumbs on both sides and place it flat on a baking sheet. Continue until the mashed potato mixture is done.
2. Prepare a big non-stick skillet or pan over medium-high heat. Fill the pan with olive oil until it is about 12 inches deep. When the oil shimmers, put the patties in a single layer in the pan. Sauté for 2 to 3 minutes on one side, or until the bottom is crunchy and golden brown, then flip and cook for another 2 to 3 minutes, watching for crispy and colour on the second side.
3. Remove the cooked mashed potato patties from the pan with a spatula and place them on a plate lined with a clean towel to drain any leftover oil.
4. Place the mashed potato patties on a serving platter and top with feta cheese and scallions. Enjoy!

Middle eastern cheese rolls

Servings: 12

Nutrition: 102 Calories, 4g Carbohydrates, 4g Protein, 8g Fat, 210mg Sodium, 11mg Cholesterol

Ingredients:

- 3 sheets phyllo dough, thawed
- Extra virgin olive oil
- ½ cup chopped fresh parsley
- 1 teaspoon fresh thyme
- 1 cup feta cheese, crumbled
- ½ cup grated Parmesan cheese
- ½ teaspoon red pepper flakes
- 2 tablespoons Extra virgin olive oil
- 2 scallions, trimmed and chopped, both white and green parts

Directions:

1. Preheat the oven to 375°F and place a rack in the center.
2. Mix the cheeses, scallions, parsley, and thyme in a medium mixing basin. Finish with the pepper flakes and a generous sprinkle of extra virgin olive oil. Put the phyllo sheets flat on a work surface and cut them into 4 equal strips with a sharp knife. Working with one phyllo strip at a time, spoon about 12 teaspoons of the feta in a straight line along the bottom edge nearest to you (leave a little space on either side for the filling to expand).
3. Roll the filling firmly 4 or 5 times away from you, tucking the sides in, so that it is now encased in a roll. Repeat with the remaining phyllo strips and filling. Coat the phyllo cheese rolls with extra virgin olive oil on the outside.

4. In a large pan, heat 14 cup olive oil until shimmering. Cook, flipping frequently, until the phyllo cheese rolls are crunchy and golden brown on all sides. Take the rolls from the heat and place them on a big dish lined with a paper towel to absorb some of the oil before serving.
5. Place the rolls on a large sheet pan in a single layer and bake for about 10 minutes, checking the rolls and flipping them over halfway through cooking, until they are crunchy and golden brown on all sides.
6. Serve the rolls warm or at room temperature on a dish.

Pizza eggplant with mushrooms

Servings: 6

Nutrition: 180 Calories, 10g Carbohydrates, 13g Protein, 11g Fat, 520mg Sodium, 38mg Cholesterol

Ingredients:

- 6 ounces sliced white mushrooms
- 2 cups fresh baby spinach
- 1 eggplant, sliced into ½-inch rounds
- Kosher salt
- 1 cup marinara sauce, store-bought
- 10 oz fresh mozzarella
- Extra virgin olive oil

Directions:

1. Preheat oven to 425°F.
2. On both sides, sprinkle the eggplant with kosher salt. If you have time, set aside the eggplant and let it rest for 20 to 30 minutes before wiping off the beads of water and any extra salt. If you don't have time, sprinkle the eggplant lightly with kosher salt before proceeding to the following step.
3. Drizzle an extra-large sheet pan with extra-virgin olive oil. Make a single layer of eggplant slices. Drizzle extra virgin olive oil generously over the top of each eggplant slice.
4. Bake for 15 to 20 minutes on the middle rack of a preheated oven, or until the eggplant is tender.
5. Next, warm 1 tablespoon extra-virgin olive oil in a saucepan. Sauté the mushrooms for about 5 minutes, stirring frequently, until they begin to brown. Whisk in the spinach for a few seconds, until it wilts. Sprinkle with kosher salt to taste.
6. When the eggplant is done, remove it from the oven and top each slice with 1 tablespoon marinara sauce and 1 slice fresh mozzarella.
7. Transfer the sheet pan to the oven and turn the temperature to broil. Broil for a few seconds, just long enough for the cheese to melt (about 1 to 2 minutes).
8. Take the eggplant out of the oven. Layer the eggplant slices with the mushroom and spinach mixture. Enjoy!

Feta croquettes with sesame and honey

Servings: 8 slices

Nutrition: 120 Calories, 15g Carbohydrates, 3g Protein, 6g Fat, 19mg Sodium, 40mg Cholesterol

Ingredients:

- ½ cup toasted sesame seeds, more as needed
- 1 8-ounce block feta
- 2 eggs
- ¼ cup all-purpose flour
- Extra virgin olive oil
- ¼ cup Honey

Directions:

1. In a small basin, crack the eggs. Add 1 to 2 tbsp water. To blend, whisk everything together.
2. Add the flour to another small bowl, then the sesame seeds to a third small bowl right next to the flour.
3. Cut the feta block into 12-inch-thick wedges.
4. Roll one piece of feta in the flour, then turn it over to ensure that all sides of the feta are coated. Put the feta in the egg mixture before rolling it in the sesame seeds. Set aside. Repeat with the remaining feta slices, coating them in the egg, flour, and sesame seeds.
5. Add enough extra virgin olive oil to a cast iron skillet to cover the bottom by about 1 inch.
6. Warm up the olive oil until it shimmers over medium-high heat. Place the feta cheese slices in the pan so that they are all touching the hot bottom. Fried till golden brown on one side, then flip and fry until golden brown and crispy on the other. To remove extra oil, place the fried feta on a tray or plate lined with paper towels.
7. Transfer the feta to a platter and sprinkle with warmed honey to serve. Serve hot.

Grilled Margherita Pizza

Servings: 5

Nutrition: 333 Calories, 43g Carbohydrates, 14g Protein, 14g Fat, 880mg Sodium, 27mg Cholesterol

Ingredients:

- ⅔ cup Olives
- 1 large garlic clove, minced
- Extra virgin olive oil
- 1-pound fresh pizza dough, store-bought or homemade, at room temperature
- 10 ounces grape tomatoes, cut into halves
- Kosher Salt
- Crushed red pepper flakes
- 1 cup packed fresh basil leaves, 10 to 15 leaves
- 6 to 8 ounces fresh mozzarella, sliced

Directions:

1. Let the dough to sit at room temperature for 1 hour if it has been refrigerated.
2. Preheat a gas to high flame.
3. Make the mixture of fresh tomatoes, basil, and olives. Put the tomatoes in a large colander and cut them into quarters. Toss with a generous teaspoon of kosher salt. For a few minutes, place the colander in a clean sink or over a bowl to drain. Add the basil, olives, and chopped garlic to a clean, dry bowl with the tomatoes. Stir with a small amount of olive oil to mix. Put aside for the time being.
4. Split the dough into two equal portions and form two pizzas on a clean floured board. Let the dough to rest for 5 minutes before reshaping to ensure that each pizza is the size you desire.
5. Put the shaped pizza dough on a pizza peel that has been lightly floured. Drizzle the top of the dough with extra virgin olive oil and place the pizza, oiled side down, right on the hot grill.
6. Close the lid and grill for 2 minutes. Spray the other side with olive oil, then flip the dough over and cook for about 2 minutes more.

7. Take the baked pizza dough from the grill and set it on a baking sheet.
8. Brush with extra olive oil and top with the mozzarella pieces. Place the pizza pan on the hot grill until the cheese has melted.
9. Remove from the grill and top with the fresh tomato mixture. Serve soon after slicing!

Delicious Greek pita with cheese and spinach

Servings: 4

Nutrition: 270 Calories, 22g Carbohydrates, 13g Protein, 15g Fat, 640mg Sodium, 30mg Cholesterol

Ingredients:
- 4 pita pockets from 2 pita loaves cut in half
- 3 ounces feta cheese
- Extra virgin olive oil
- 3 heaping cups baby spinach
- 3 to 4 ounces fresh mozzarella cheese sliced into ¼-inch slices
- ⅓ cup sundried tomatoes packed in oil drained, chopped
- ¼ to ⅓ cup basil pesto

Directions:

1. Put 1 tablespoon extra-virgin olive oil, heated in a grill pan over medium-high heat until shimmering. Cook for a few minutes, stirring occasionally, until the spinach has wilted. Remove the spinach to a platter and turn off the heat. Open the pita pockets. Put the feta on the bottom, then the basil pesto. Top with a bit of the wilted spinach. Combine the mozzarella and sundried tomatoes in a mixing bowl. Return the grill pan to medium-high heat. Brush both sides of the pitas with extra virgin olive oil. Place the pita sandwiches in the preheated pan, making sure that they all contact.
2. Heat for 1 to 2 minutes on one side, exerting pressure with the back of a spatula to the top of the sandwich, then flip and cook for another few minutes, putting pressure with your spatula again, until the cheese is melted, and the bread has some nice char lines. Regulate the heat so that the bread is crispy but not burned and the mozzarella is melted.
3. Serve right away!

Spanish bruschetta with tomato

Servings: 10 slices

Nutrition: 111 Calories, 23g Carbohydrates, 4g Protein, 1g Fat, 222mg Sodium, 3mg Cholesterol

Ingredients:
- 3 tomatoes, large and very ripe tomatoes are best, I used heirloom tomatoes
- Extra virgin olive oil
- 1 loaf ciabatta bread
- sea salt, or kosher salt
- splash of fresh lime juice
- 1 to 2 garlic cloves, sliced in half

Directions:

1. Set your oven to broil and place a rack about 6 inches away from the heat source.
2. Cut the loaf of bread in half lengthwise, then into 2-inch slices. Drizzle the bread with extra virgin olive oil and place it on a baking sheet. Toast for 3 minutes in a hot oven, 6 inches from the broiler, or until the bread is softly golden brown.
3. Snip a little piece from the tip of the tomatoes and grate them through the big holes of a box grater. Remove the peels and set aside. Sprinkle the tomato puree with salt and lime juice, if desired.
4. When the bread is done, massage the garlic cloves over it, then arrange the grated tomatoes on top. Serve.

Yummy cauliflower fritters with mint yogurt

Servings: 16 fritters

Nutrition: 180 calories, 10g Carbohydrates, 4g Protein, 1g Fat, 190mg Sodium, 22mg Cholesterol

Ingredients:

- 2 tablespoon lemon juice
- 1 tablespoon olive oil
- 1 cup Greek yogurt
- ½ teaspoon dried mint
- ½ teaspoon salt
- 2 eggs
- 1 ½ teaspoon cumin
- ¾ teaspoon ground cinnamon
- ½ teaspoon turmeric
- ½ teaspoon red pepper flakes
- 1 small cauliflower, cut into 1 ½-inch florets (3 cups florets)
- 1 cup all-purpose flour
- Kosher salt and black pepper
- 1 cup sunflower oil
- 1 cup fresh parsley, finely chopped
- 1 small onion, finely chopped
- ½ teaspoon baking powder

Directions:

1. To create the mint yogurt, combine the first 5 ingredients in a bowl. Stir everything together and place in the fridge until ready to serve.
2. Bring a medium saucepan of salted water to a boil over high heat, then add the cauliflower. Cook for 4 minutes, then strain into a colander (reserving 3 to 4 tablespoons of the cooking water).
3. Crush the cauliflower with a fork or a potato masher, then transfer it to a large mixing bowl.
4. Mix in the flour, parsley, onion, eggs, cumin, cinnamon, turmeric, pepper flakes, baking powder, 14 salt, and black pepper to taste. Mix in 3 tablespoons of the cooking water thoroughly.
5. Paper towels should be used to line a large dish.
6. Warm the oil in a big sauté pan (approximately 9 inches wide). When the oil is hot, carefully pour in 2 to 3 teaspoons of batter per fritter. To avoid filling too much the pan, work in groups (putting maximum 4 fritters at a time) and use a spatula to keep them apart. Fried for 4–5 minutes, flipping halfway through, or until both sides are golden brown.
7. Put the fried fritters to the ready plate using a slotted spoon and leave aside while you proceed with the remaining batches.
8. With the mint yogurt on the side, serve hot or at room temperature.

Ingredients:

- 3 oz Feta cheese, sliced into slabs
- 1 English cucumber, thinly sliced into rounds
- 1 bell pepper (any color), thinly sliced into rounds
- 1 vine-ripe tomato, thinly sliced into rounds
- 5 radishes, thinly sliced into rounds
- 4 eggs, soft boiled
- Kosher salt
- 1 small red onion, thinly sliced into rounds
- 1 lemon, cut into wedges
- 12 oz smoked salmon
- 4 oz Cream cheese
- Red pepper flakes
- ¼ cup assorted olives
- ⅓ cup marinated artichoke hearts

Aperitif with salmon and mix of vegetables

Servings: 6

Nutrition: 200 Calories, 10g Carbohydrates, 20g Protein, 3g Fat, 30mg Sodium, 130mg Cholesterol

Directions:

1. Bring the eggs to a boil. Bring a pot of water to a boil over moderate heat, making sure it can accommodate all the eggs in one layer. Carefully lower the eggs into the boiling water using a spoon. Cook for 612 minutes, reducing the heat as needed to keep a slow boil. When the eggs are done, place them in a big dish of ice water and let aside for 2 minutes. Peel and cut the eggs in half, then sprinkle with kosher salt and a pinch of red pepper flakes.

2. To make the salmon plate, fill one-third of the platter with a small bowl of cream cheese. Put the feta cheese in a different corner of the dish. Surround the cheese with the salmon, cucumbers, bell peppers, tomatoes, radish, onions, olives, artichoke hearts, and lemon wedges. Add extra red pepper flakes to taste.
3. Serve with crackers or crostini of your choice.

Bruschetta with feta and salmon

Servings: 4

Nutrition: 155 Calories, 17g Carbohydrates, 13g Protein, 4g Fat, 540mg Sodium, 16mg Cholesterol

Ingredients:

- Kosher salt, to taste
- 1 lime or lemon
- Extra virgin olive oil
- 1 small beet, peeled and cut into thin, short sticks
- 1 carrot, peeled and cut into thin, short sticks
- 3 radishes, cut into thin, short sticks
- 2 ounces quality feta cheese
- 5 to 6 ounces quality smoked salmon fillet
- 1 green onion, white and green parts, sliced into rounds
- 4 slices whole wheat bread, toasted

Directions:

1. Mix the carrots, radish, green onion, and beets in a small bowl. Sprinkle with kosher salt. Toss with a healthy squeeze of lime and a sprinkle of extra virgin olive oil.
2. Mix the feta cheese with a drizzle of olive oil and crush it with the back of a fork to make it easier to spread.
3. Sprinkle some feta on each slice of toasted bread. Garnish with the smoked salmon and serve with a squeeze of lime, if desired.

Stuffed zucchini slices with feta and tomato

Servings: 6

Nutrition: 52 Calories, 6g Carbohydrates, 4g Protein, 2g Fat, 15mg Sodium, 7mg Cholesterol

Ingredients:

- 6 oz cherry tomatoes sliced in halves
- 3 green onions both white and green parts, ends trimmed, chopped
- ½ cup crumbled feta cheese more to your liking
- 3 zucchini trimmed and sliced length-wise into halves
- extra virgin olive oil
- Zest of 1 lemon
- Splash lemon juice
- Kosher salt and pepper to your liking
- Dried oregano large sprinkle
- 6 to 10 fresh mint leaves chopped
- Large handful fresh parsley chopped

Directions:

1. Over medium heat, warm a cast iron skillet.
2. Massage the sides of the zucchini with extra virgin olive oil. Sprinkle zucchini with salt, freshly ground pepper, and oregano, focusing on the flesh side.
3. Put the zucchini on the hot grill, flesh side down. Grill for 3 to 5 minutes, or until soft and attractively browned on the front side, then turn and grill for another 3 to 5 minutes, or until the back side is also soft and gets color.
4. Take the zucchini from the fire and set aside until cool enough to handle.
5. To make zucchini boats, scoop out the flesh using a tiny spoon (do not discard). Squeeze out all of the juice from the zucchini flesh.

6. Stuff the zucchini boats with the filling. In a mixing dish, combine the zucchini flesh, cherry tomatoes, green onions, feta, mint, parsley, and lemon zest. Add a little of of lemon juice and little more oregano to taste. Stir everything together and sprinkle with extra virgin olive oil.
7. Stuff the zucchini boats with the filling mixture and put on a serving plate. Enjoy!

Greek fried eggplant sticks

Servings: 6

Nutrition: 125 Calories, 3g Fat, 22g Carbohydrates, 6g Protein, 63mg Sodium, 5mg Cholesterol

Ingredients:
- 1 cup breadcrumbs
- 1 tsp garlic powder
- 1 medium eggplant
- ¾ cup all-purpose flour
- Pinch salt and pepper
- Olive oil cooking spray
- 2 eggs, lightly beaten
- 1 tsp dried oregano

Directions:
1. Set the oven temperature to 425 degrees Fahrenheit.
2. To begin, slice the eggplant into 1-inch rounds. Let aside for 20 minutes to allow the eggplant to sweat away any acidity. Let to air dry. Cut the eggplant slices into uniform batons or "fries."
3. Coat the eggplant fries in flour. Soak them in the eggs, then in a combination of breadcrumbs, garlic powder, oregano, salt, and pepper.
4. Place a wire rack on top of a baking tray and set aside. Cooking spray olive oil on the wire rack. Place the eggplant fries on top of the wire rack now. Coat the eggplant fries with olive oil cooking spray.
5. Bake for 10 minutes, or until the eggplant fries are browned and crunchy, in a 425°F oven.
6. Serve the eggplant fries immediately.

Mini bruschetta with figs and goat cheese

Servings: 10

Nutrition: 250 Calories, 15g Fat, 25g Carbohydrates, 7g Protein, 116mg Sodium, 10mg Cholesterol

Ingredients:
- ¼ cup shelled pistachios, crushed
- ¼ cup walnut hearts, crushed
- 2 tbsp molasses, more for later
- 10 slices baguette
- Extra virgin olive oil
- pinch salt and pepper
- 5 ripe mission figs, halved
- 6 oz goat cheese
- 20 basil leaves, torn

Directions:
1. Set the broiler to high heat and position the rack 6 inches below the element.
2. Rub both sides of the baguette slices with olive oil. Place the baguette pieces on a baking pan and set aside. Broil for a few minutes, or until the top is golden brown and caramelized (about 2-3 minutes). Take it out of the oven but leave the broiler on.
3. Mix the goat cheese, crushed pistachios and walnuts, molasses, basil leaves, salt, and pepper in a mixing bowl. Using a spoon, thoroughly blend the goat cheese mixture.
4. Garnish each toasted baguette slice with a large portion of the goat cheese mixture and a piece of fig.
5. Put the goat cheese crostini in a serving plate once cool enough to handle. Sprinkle with molasses and top with fresh basil, if desired. Enjoy at hot or at room temperature.
6. Place the crostini back in the oven. Broil for 3-4 minutes more, or until the goat cheese is melted and caramelized around the sides. The figs will soften and color little more. Switch off the broiler and remove from the oven.

Sticks of meat with feta cheese

Servings: 16

Nutrition: 300 Calories, 22g Fat, 16g Carbohydrates, 13g Protein, 303mg Sodium, 13mg Cholesterol

Ingredients:

- 1 small yellow onion, finely chopped
- Salt and pepper
- 1 lb ground beef
- 1 tbsp olive oil, plus 1 cup for later
- 1 cup shredded mozzarella cheese
- 2 eggs
- 5 oz creamy feta cheese
- 1 tsp dill weed
- 1 tbsp olive oil
- 16-20 Phyllo sheets
- 1 egg, mixed with little water

Directions:

1. Set the oven temperature to 400°F.
2. In a skillet, heat 1 tablespoon olive oil. Sauté the onions quickly over medium-high heat.
3. Mix in the ground meat and seasonings. Simmer, tossing periodically, until the ground beef is fully cooked and browned (about 8 minutes). Let to cool slightly.
4. When the ground beef has cooled, mix it with the remaining filling ingredients.
5. Place 16 phyllo pastry sheets, or more, if necessary, in a big tray. Cover with a dampened kitchen towel.
6. Place two sheets of phyllo on a large chopping board. Brush the phyllo with olive oil generously. Cut along the centre with a sharp knife to produce two long phyllo strips.
7. Start with one phyllo strip and make your first roll. Put a tablespoon of the meat-cheese mixture on the short end of each phyllo strip. Two times, roll away from you.
8. Fold the phyllo strip sides in all the way, next roll the phyllo toward the other end.
9. Drizzle with additional olive oil and egg wash. Put the first phyllo roll on a large baking sheet that has been lightly greased. Rep with the second phyllo strip.
10. Keep going with the remaining phyllo sheets, working with two at a time. You should finish up with 16 perfectly lined up phyllo dough meat rolls on your large baking sheet.
11. Preheat the oven to 400 degrees Fahrenheit. Bake for 15 minutes.
12. Remove from the oven. Serve warm.

Tasty Greek skewers

Servings: 6

Ingredients:

- ½ English cucumber, halved lengthwise, then sliced into half moons
- 1 small green pepper, cored, cut into 10 to 12 square pieces
- 6 ounces creamy feta cheese, cut into 10 to 12 cubes
- 10 to 12 cherry or grape tomatoes
- 10 to 12 pitted Kalamata olives
- 1 tablespoon red wine vinegar
- 1 tablespoon extra-virgin olive oil
- 1 garlic clove, minced
- ½ lime, juice
- Kosher salt and black pepper
- 1 teaspoon dried oregano

Nutrition: 125 Calories, 5g Carbohydrates, 5g Protein, 10g Fat, 530mg Sodium, 25mg Cholesterol

Directions:

1. Make 10–12 tiny bamboo skewers. Line one skewer with one feta cube, a piece of cucumber, a slice of green pepper, one cherry tomato, and one kalamata olives at the top. Continue until you have 10 to 12 little feta and veggie skewers.
2. Combine the garlic, lime juice, and red wine vinegar in a small bowl. Sprinkle with kosher salt, black pepper, and dried oregano to taste. While mixing, add in the extra virgin olive oil and continue whisking.
3. Place the skewers on a serving plate and drizzle with the dressing. Serve immediately or store in the refrigerator for later.

Desserts

Special olive oil chocolate cake

Servings: 10

Nutrition: 385 Calories, 38g Carbohydrates, 5g Protein, 25g Fat, 316mg Sodium, 70mg Cholesterol

Ingredients:

- ½ cup (42g) natural cocoa powder
- ½ teaspoon cinnamon
- 3 large eggs
- ¾ cup (193ml) extra-virgin olive oil
- 1 ¼ cup (167g) all-purpose flour
- ½ teaspoon baking soda
- 1 cup (200g) organic cane sugar
- Fresh berries
- ½ teaspoon baking soda
- 1 teaspoon kosher salt
- ½ cup plus 2 tablespoons (106ml) water
- 2 teaspoons vanilla extract
- 1 teaspoon almond extract

Directions:

1. Set the oven temperature to 325 degrees Fahrenheit. Line a 9-inch round cake pan with parchment paper and drizzle with olive oil.
2. Sift flour, baking soda, and salt together in a large mixing bowl.
3. In a small saucepan, mix 12 cup + 2 teaspoons water, chocolate, and cinnamon and bring to a simmer. Take the pot from the heat. Mix in the chocolate powder and cinnamon until combined.
4. On medium-high speed, mix together eggs, sugar, extracts and olive oil, in a stand mixer equipped with a hand mixer for about 4 minutes.
5. Put cocoa powder mixture to egg mixture and beat on moderate speed until barely combined, scraping down the sides and bottom of the bowl as needed. Mix in the flour mixture until just combined.
6. Put the cake batter in the prepared pan on the center rack of the oven. 35-40 minutes in the oven. When a tester pushed into the center comes away with only a few damp crumbs adhering to it, the cake is done. Let the cake to cool on a wire rack for at least 1 hour. Invert the cooled cake onto a dish by running a butter knife over the edge. Remove the top layer of parchment paper with care.
7. Beat the heavy cream, Greek yogurt, and powdered sugar on medium to medium high with a hand mixer or in the bowl of a stand mixer equipped with the whisk attachment until soft peaks form.
8. Serve the cake with a scoop of Greek yogurt whip and fresh berries. Serve right away!

Traditional cannoli

Servings: 24

Nutrition: 120 Calories, 18g Carbohydrates, 3g Protein, 5g Fat, 24mg Sodium, 26mg Cholesterol

Ingredients:

- 4-5 tablespoons unsalted butter, cut into small pieces
- 2 eggs, beaten
- 3 tablespoons Marsala wine
- 2 cups all-purpose flour, more as needed
- pinch salt
- Oil for frying
- Confectioners' sugar for dusting
- 1 egg white, lightly beaten mixed with 1 tablespoon of water
- 3 tablespoons sugar
- ¾ cup confectioners' sugar
- ½ teaspoon cinnamon
- 2 ounces dark chocolate, grated, more for dusting
- 12 ounces whole milk ricotta cheese
- 3 ounces chopped candied fruit

Directions:

1. In a large mixing basin, sift together the flour, salt, and sugar. Massage in the butter with your hands until you have a gritty mixture. Incorporate the egg and Marsala wine. Put the dough out onto a lightly floured work area and knead by hand until smooth. Return the dough to the bowl and put it in the fridge while you prepare the filling. Mix the grated chocolate, ricotta cheese, confectioners' sugar, and candied fruit in a mixing bowl. Stir everything together with a fork or a hand mixer until everything is fully blended. Put aside for the for a while.
2. Remove the pastry dough from the refrigerator. Roll out the pastry dough until it is very thin (about 18' thin) on a clean, lightly dusted work surface. Slice the dough into rounds with a 3-inch round cookie cutter or a drinking glass. You should have anywhere from 18 to 24 rounds.
3. Flour 6 cannoli molds and loosely wrap each pastry round around a cannoli mold. Soften the dough's sides with the egg wash and press to hold the edges firmly in the center, using just a small amount of the egg wash to make sure the dough does not open when baked.
4. Fill a tiny cooking pot approximately a third of the way with oil. Preheat the oil to 350°F. Deep fried the cannoli pastry shells until they are brown and crisp. Remove from the oil with tongs or a big, slotted spoon and set on a dish lined with paper towels. After the pastry shells have cooled sufficiently, twist the cannoli forms to release the shells.
5. Keep going with the cannoli molds until all the cannoli have been cooked.
6. When the cannoli shells are cool enough to handle, pipe or spoon the filling inside. Sprinkle with confectioner's sugar and a small amount of grated dark chocolate. Enjoy

Mediterranean lemon cheesecake

Servings: 10

Nutrition: 385 Calories, 30g Carbohydrates, 20g Protein, 22g Fat, 165mg Sodium, 200mg Cholesterol

Ingredients:

- 1 ¼ cup sugar
- 1 teaspoon vanilla extract
- 3 pounds whole milk ricotta cheese
- 8 large eggs
- Zest of 3 lemons
- Olive oil to coat the pan

Directions:

1. Set the oven temperature to 425 degrees Fahrenheit.
2. Remove the ricotta cheese from the liquid and set aside.
3. Add the cheese, eggs, sugar, vanilla essence, and lemon zest to the bowl of a standing mixer fitted with a blade. For 10 minutes, mix on low and gradually increase to medium-low speed. The mixture will appear light and fluffy, similar to a batter. Keep the speed of a hand mixer low. If using a wooden spoon, continue to stir until the mixture is frothy.
4. Olive oil the bottom and sides of a 9" springform pan. Put the springform pan on a large baking sheet.
5. Spoon the batter into the springform pan and shake it gently.
6. Cook for 30 minutes at 425°F, then decrease the temperature to 375°F and bake for another 40 minutes, or until the batter has mostly firmed up and the top of the cake has turned a wonderful golden-brown color.
7. Let the cake to cool completely (1 to 2 hours), then cover with plastic wrap and place in the refrigerator for at least 6 hours. It's better to refrigerate the cake overnight if you have the time).
8. After the cake has completely chilled, take it from the springform pan. Cut and serve! If desired, sprinkle a little additional lemon zest over each slice.

Homemade yogurt

Servings: 6

Nutrition: 150 Calories, 33g Carbohydrates, 4g Protein, 1g Fat, 14mg Sodium, 2mg Cholesterol

Ingredients:

- 1 cup Whole milk Greek yogurt
- 2 teaspoon orange extract, or vanilla extract
- 4 cups sliced frozen strawberries, or other frozen fruit of your choice
- 2 cups sliced frozen banana
- ¼ cup sugar
- 1 tablespoon corn syrup
- 4 to 6 tablespoon honey

Directions:

1. In the container of a blender fitted with a blade, combine the frozen strawberries, banana, yogurt, orange extract (or vanilla extract), honey, sugar, and corn syrup.
2. Mix everything together until it forms a creamy smoothie-like consistency. If you like it sweeter, add a little extra honey.
3. Smooth the surface of the mixture in a freezer-safe container. Place a piece of paper to the top of the yogurt to avoid ice crystals from forming. Freeze for at least 6 hours or overnight. Let the frozen yogurt to soften for a few minutes at room temperature before eating, just until it is soft enough to scoop. Scoop out the desired quantity.

Tahini banana milkshake

Servings: 3

Nutrition: 300 calories, 12g Fat, 48g Carbohydrates, 6g Protein, 101mg Sodium, 0mg Cholesterol

Ingredients:

- ¼ cup tahini
- ¼ cup crushed ice
- 2 frozen bananas, sliced
- 4 pitted dates
- 1 ½ cups unsweetened almond milk
- Pinch ground cinnamon

Directions:

1. In a processor, combine the sliced frozen bananas and the additional ingredients. Blend until the mixture is creamy and silky.
2. Pour the banana date shakes to serving cups and top with a pinch of ground cinnamon. Enjoy!

Fig dessert

Servings: 4

Nutrition: 700 Calories, 50g Fat, 47g Carbohydrates, 14g Protein, 260mg Sodium, 10mg Cholesterol

Ingredients:

- 4-5 oz goat cheese, room temperature
- ¼ cup walnuts, roughly chopped
- 1 sheet of good store-bought puff pastry, thawed in fridge for 3 hours or so
- 8 oz fresh black mission figs
- 1 tbsp butter, melted
- ¼ cup fresh mint leaves, roughly chopped
- 2 tbsp good fig jam

Directions:

1. The oven should be heated to 375 degrees Fahrenheit.
2. Put four approximately equal rectangular pieces of frozen puff pastry on a baking sheet coated with parchment paper.
3. On each piece, spread goat cheese. Next add the jam, figs, and walnuts.
4. Glaze figs and puff pastry edges with melted butter.
5. Turn the pastry edges up slightly.
6. Bake for 18-20 minutes at 375°F, or until the pastry is golden and fluffy.
7. If preferred, top with minced mint leaves and more walnuts.

Carrot cake with honey

Servings: 12

Nutrition: 170 Calories, 9g Fat, 5g Protein, 20g Carbohydrates, 140mg Sodium, 7mg Cholesterol

Ingredients:

- 2 ¼ cup whole wheat flour
- 1 ½ tsp baking powder
- ½ tsp salt
- 4 tsp ground cinnamon
- ½ tsp ground cardamom
- ½ cup extra virgin olive oil
- ½ cup Greek yogurt
- ⅓ cup chopped walnuts
- powdered sugar for light dusting
- ⅓ cup milk (2% reduced fat milk)
- ½ cup quality dark honey
- 3 eggs
- ¼ tsp ground ginger
- 2 cups finely grated carrots
- 6 dates, pitted and finely chopped

Directions:

1. Set the oven temperature to 350°F.
2. Combine together the olive oil, geek yogurt, and milk in a large mixing dish. Whisk together the eggs one at a time.
3. In the meantime, combine together the flour, baking powder, salt, and spices.
4. Mix the dry ingredients into the wet ingredients slowly with a wooden spoon.
5. Incorporate the carrots. Stir well, then add the dates and walnuts. Mix with the wooden spoon once more until well blended.
6. Cover a 9-inch square baking pan with parchment paper. Fill the pan halfway with carrot cake batter. Cook 1 hour in a preheated oven at 350 degrees F. Let to cool completely. If preferred, top with powdered sugar. Cut the dough into 9 or 12 square pieces. Enjoy!

Orange cake with pistachios

Servings: 15

Nutrition: 380 Calories, 11g Fat, 66g Carbohydrates, 8g Protein, 31mg Sodium, 7mg Cholesterol

Ingredients:

- zest of 1 lemon
- zest of 1 orange
- 1 ¼ cup all-purpose flour
- 1 cup coarse semolina
- 5 large eggs
- 1 cup low-fat Greek yogurt
- ¾ cup plus 1 tablespoon extra virgin olive oil
- Handful shaved almonds for topping
- 2 cups granulated sugar
- 5 tbsp ground almonds
- 2 tsp baking powder
- 1 ¼ cup quality runny honey
- juice of 2 oranges
- 1 1/4 cup shelled salted pistachios
- juice of 1 lemon

Directions:

1. Prepare the oven for 350 degrees Fahrenheit.
2. Butter a baking pan and dust with flour (shake it to get an equal coating of flour).
3. Prepare the cake batter. In a large mixing bowl, combine all of the cake ingredients (not yet the shaved almonds). To mix, use a wooden spoon or a whisk.
4. Spread the batter uniformly in the prepared baking pan using a spatula.
5. Bake for 25 to 30 minutes, or until brown and well done. To be sure, stick a wooden skewer into the middle of the cake; if the cake is cooked, it should come out clean.
6. Remove from the oven and leave the cake to cool in the pan.
7. Start preparing the honey syrup after the cake has cooled. Pistachios should be toasted on a dry non-stick pan over low to medium heat. Mix in the honey once they begin to smell. Pour in the orange and lemon juices. Bring to a boil for 1–2 minutes, or until syrupy.

8. To make holes in the cake, stab it with a small knife or a skewer all over. Spread the honey pistachio syrup as equally as possible over the cake. If necessary, spread the pistachios around the top of the cake with a spoon. If used, top with shaved almonds.
9. You can serve the cake in 12 to 15 squares.

French toast with honey and orange

Servings: 5

Nutrition: 560 Calories, 93g Carbohydrates, 20g Protein, 13g Fat, 613mg Sodium, 255mg Cholesterol

Ingredients:

- ¼ cup orange juice
- 2 oranges, zested
- ½ cup honey
- 1 ¾ teaspoon ground cinnamon
- 1 teaspoon almond extract
- ¼ teaspoon kosher salt
- 1 loaf challah bread, about 8 to 10 thick slices
- 6 eggs
- 1 cup blueberries
- 4 tablespoons creme fraiche
- 1 cup whole milk
- 4 teaspoons granulated sugar

Directions:

1. Save aside the zest from each orange. Remove the top and bottom of an orange to create a flat surface on which to work and reveal the orange's flesh. Begin at the top and work your way down, slicing between the orange flesh and the white pith. Do this all the way around the orange until no peel or pith remains.
2. Carefully separate each section from the membrane and put on a small plate while keeping the orange over a medium bowl to capture any liquids. Rep with the other orange. After segmenting each orange, press the membranes to release any juices into the bowl.
3. Put 12 cup honey and 14 cup orange juice from when you squeezed the oranges in a small pot set over medium low heat. Cook the mixture, stirring occasionally, until it is mixed and pourable. Place in a small container.
4. Cut the loaf into 12-inch-thick wedges. According to the dimensions of your loaf, you should finish up with 8 to 10 slices.
5. Using a fork, beat the eggs, orange zest, almond extract, cinnamon, milk, salt, and sugar in a plate or in a bowl.
6. Fill the dish with custard with as many slices as will fit in a single layer. Turn them over to cover both sides. In a skillet over medium heat, melt 2 tablespoons butter. As it begins to sizzle, add the moistened bread in a single layer. Fry until golden brown on one side, then flip and cook until golden brown on the other. On a plate, put 2 slices of French toast. Garnish with 1 tablespoon cream fraiche, berries, and orange slices on top. End up serving with the orange honey syrup drizzled on top.

Olive oil orange cake

Servings: 12

Nutrition: 370 Calories, 44g Carbohydrates, 4g Fat, 20g Fat, 280mg Sodium, 44mg Cholesterol

Ingredients:

- ¼ teaspoon baking soda
- ¾ to 1 teaspoon ground cardamom
- 1 ½ cups plus 2 Tablespoons granulated sugar
- 1 cup extra-virgin olive oil
- 2 cups all-purpose flour, plus more for the pan
- 1 ¼ cups whole milk
- 2 tablespoons sifted confectioners' sugar, for garnish
- 1 teaspoon kosher salt
- 1 teaspoon baking powder
- 3 large eggs
- Grated zest of 2 oranges, plus 2 tablespoons fresh orange juice

Directions:

1. Set the oven to 350°F and position a rack in the middle.
2. Grease a 9-inch circular cake pan with olive oil on the bottom and sides. Cover the bottom of the pan with parchment paper and dust with a little flour, shaking off the excess.
3. Combine the following dry ingredients: In a medium mixing basin, combine 2 cups flour, salt, baking powder, and baking soda.
4. Mix the 1 1/2 cup granulated sugar, cardamom, and eggs in a large mixing bowl. Beat the mixture with an electric hand mixer on high for 5 minutes, or until thick and fluffy. While the mixer is running, sprinkle in the olive oil gently and beat until combined.
5. Lower the speed to low and add half of the orange zest, half of the orange juice, and half of the milk. Mix until smooth.
6. Incorporate the flour mixture into the wet ingredients on low until you have a homogenous batter.
7. Pour the cake batter into the prepared pan and sprinkle with the other 2 tablespoons granulated sugar on top. Bake for 40–45 minutes, or until the center is firm and a skewer inserted into the middle comes out dry.
8. Let the cake to cool in the pan for 30 minutes, then run a tiny knife down the edge, invert onto a big dish, and invert again onto a rack to cool fully.
9. Sprinkle the cake with powdered sugar and garnish with orange zest before serving.

Middle Eastern style ice cream with pistachios

Servings: 4

Nutrition: 770 Calories, 85g Carbohydrates, 12g Protein, 45g Fat, 200mg Sodium, 60mg Cholesterol

Ingredients:

- ½ cup crushed pistachios
- ½ teaspoon ground cinnamon
- ¼ cup extra-virgin olive oil
- 4-6 sheets phyllo dough, torn into pieces
- 1 large tub (8 scoops) vanilla ice cream
- ½ cup honey warmed
- ½ cup crushed walnuts
- 1 tablespoon brown sugar

Directions:

1. Warm 14 cup oil in a small saucepan on medium-high heat until shimmering. When the oil starts to shimmer, add the phyllo and cook, rotating occasionally, until crunchy and golden brown on both sides. Place the crispy phyllo to a big paper towel-lined dish lined with paper towels to drain any leftover oil.
2. Mix the walnuts, pistachios, cinnamon, and brown sugar in a small mixing dish.
3. Fill four tiny serving cups halfway with the crispy phyllo. Add one scoop of ice cream, a tablespoon of the nut mixture, and a sprinkle of warmed honey on top.

4. Repeat with the remaining crispy phyllo, finishing with a scoop of ice cream, additional nuts, and a sprinkle of honey. Serve right away.

Sweet pumpkin parfait

Servings: 6

Nutrition: 145 Calories, 20g Carbohydrates, 6g Protein, 4g Fat, 35mg Sodium, 10mg Cholesterol

Ingredients:

- 3-4 tablespoons mascarpone cheese
- 1 tablespoon vanilla extract
- 1 15-ounce can pumpkin puree, or scant 2 cups homemade pumpkin puree
- 1 ¼ cup Greek yogurt
- 1 ½-2 teaspoons ground cinnamon
- ¼ teaspoon nutmeg
- 2 ½ tablespoons brown sugar
- Chocolate chips for garnish
- 2 tablespoons honey or molasses, more for garnish
- Chopped hazelnuts or walnuts for garnish

Directions:

1. In a big mixing container, combine the pumpkin puree, Greek yogurt, and all of the rest of the ingredients, except the chocolate chips and nuts. Mix everything together with a hand electric mixer or a whisk until it's smooth.
2. Taste it and adapt the flavor to your liking, for example, by adding a little more molasses or brown sugar to sweeten it up. Alternatively, if you want extra cinnamon or nutmeg, alter the spices. Blend once more to combine.
3. Pour the pumpkin-yogurt mixture into small (3-ounce) goblets or mason jars. Put it in the fridge for 30 minutes or overnight, covered.
4. When it's time to serve, sprinkle each with molasses and sprinkle with chocolate chips and crushed hazelnuts or walnuts. Enjoy!

Greek yogurt with dried fruit

Servings: 4

Nutrition: 670 Calories, 35g Fat, 60g Carbohydrates, 23g Protein, 70mg Sodium, 5mg Cholesterol

Ingredients:

- 4 tbsp Kahlua, divided
- 1 tsp vanilla extract
- 1 tsp cinnamon
- 3 cups fat free Greek Yogurt
- 1 cup light whipped cream
- ½ cup pistachios, shelled, chopped
- ½ cup hazelnuts, shelled, chopped
- ½ cup sugar
- ½ cup raisins

Directions:

1. Mix raisins and two tablespoons Kahlua rum in a small microwave-safe bowl. Microwave on high for 50 seconds. Continue to the microwave for another 30 seconds, stirring halfway through. The raisins will have absorbed the Kahlua and will be beautiful and plump. Set aside your seat.
2. Pistachios and hazelnuts should be roughly chopped in a blender.
3. With a hand mixer, combine Greek yogurt, whipped cream, sugar, two tablespoons Kahlua, vanilla extract, and cinnamon in a large mixing basin.
4. At this stage, cover and chill the yogurt mixture for an hour or until ready to assemble.
5. To start, put two to three tablespoons of the yogurt mixture into the bottom of a serving glass.
6. Put the mixed nuts and Kahlua raisins on top.
7. Finish with one tablespoon of the yogurt mixture and a sprinkle of nuts.

Traditional apple strudel

Servings: 10

Nutrition: 130 Calories, 22g Carbohydrates, 3g Protein, 2g Fat, 20mg Sodium, 3mg Cholesterol

Ingredients:

- 1 teaspoon ground cinnamon
- ¼ teaspoon nutmeg
- ¼ teaspoon ground cardamom
- 4 tablespoon orange juice
- 2 teaspoon ghee clarified butter
- 2 tablespoon extra virgin olive oil
- ⅓ cup raisins
- 10 thawed phyllo dough sheets
- 3 apples, peeled, cored, thinly sliced
- ¼ cup brown sugar
- ½ cup chopped walnuts

Directions:

1. Set the oven temperature to 375°F.
2. Prepare the filling. Ghee and extra virgin olive oil are heated in a big skillet. Combine the sliced apples, orange juice, nutmeg, cardamom and brown sugar in a mixing bowl. Cook, stirring occasionally, for about 2 minutes over medium heat. Mix in the walnuts and raisins. Take from the heat and leave aside for a few minutes.
3. Cover a big sheet pan with parchment paper. In a small bowl, combine the apple stuffing juices with a bit more extra virgin olive oil.
4. Place 10 to 12 phyllo sheets flat on a clean surface.
5. Place one phyllo sheet in the sheet pan. Sprinkle with the prepared mixture (apple filling juice and olive oil) and some brown sugar.
6. Continue with the rest of the phyllo sheets.
7. Next, with the sheet pan horizontally arranged, spoon the apple mixture towards the center, leaving a 2-inch border of phyllo all around. Fold the phyllo's short edges to cover 2 inches of apple mixture on each end. Apply extra virgin olive oil to the ends. Wrap the phyllo over the apple mixture and wrap towards the other end, beginning with the long edge closest to you. Maintain the bottom seam.
8. Drizzle extra virgin olive oil over the strudel. Bake for 35 minutes on the middle rack of a preheated oven, or until the phyllo is golden brown.
9. Remove from the oven and cool on the baking sheet. To serve, sprinkle the apple strudel with confectioner's sugar and top with any extra walnuts or raisins. Cut into slices and serve.

Mini bruschetta with Greek yogurt and peaches

Servings: 10

Ingredients:

- Pinch ground nutmeg
- Pinch ground cinnamon
- 3 peaches, cored and sliced into thin wedges
- ⅓ cup Greek yogurt
- 6 oz cream cheese, softened
- ¼ cup roughly chopped pecan halves
- Honey to drizzle
- zest of one orange
- ⅓ cup sugar
- 3 tbsp orange juice
- 8-10 crostini, French baguette slices, toasted

Nutrition: 200 Calories, 9g Fat, 28g Carbohydrates, 4g Protein, 58mg Sodium, 5mg Cholesterol

Directions:

1. Blend the Greek yogurt, cream cheese, orange zest, sugar, nutmeg, and cinnamon in a blender. Mix the mixture until it is well combined and fluffy. In a mixing dish, combine the beaten Greek yogurt and the honey. Put it in the fridge for one hour, or until ready to use.
2. Set the oven temperature to 425 degrees Fahrenheit.
3. In a mixing dish, combine the peaches and orange juice. Put the peaches on a baking sheet lined with parchment paper and lightly pat them dry. Preheat the oven to 425°F and bake for 20-25 minutes.

4. After the whipped Greek yogurt mixture is finished, generously distribute it over the toasted bruschetta. Serve with minced pecans and two roasted peach slices. Pour a small amount of honey over each bruschetta. Enjoy!

28-Day Meal Plan

Monday	Week 1	Week 2
Breakfast	Bowl of oats with banana and chocolate	Nutritious spinach crepes
Lunch	Vegetarian ravioli with artichokes	Greek pasta with feta
Dinner	Orange and pomegranate salad	Sticks of meat with feta cheese
Tuesday		
Breakfast	Toast with egg and avocado with oriental flavours	Avocado Cheese Omelette
Lunch	Vegetarian fettuccine with mushrooms	Mediterranean brown rice
Dinner	Fresh fruit salad	Mini bruschetta with figs and goat cheese
Wednesday		
Breakfast	Greek yogurt scrambled eggs	Nectarine peach bruschetta
Lunch	Mediterranean Chicken Soup	Traditional Chicken Parmesan pasta
Dinner	Feta croquettes with sesame and honey	Salad with watermelon and feta
Thursday		
Breakfast	Avocado Cheese Omelette	Bruschetta with Greek yogurt and tomatoes
Lunch	Beef ribs in wine with potatoes	Italian fish soup
Dinner	Greek fried eggplant sticks	Grilled Margherita Pizza
Friday		
Breakfast	Bruschetta with spinach, squash and egg	Nectarine peach bruschetta
Lunch	Summer pasta salad	Delicious cod with lemon
Dinner	Pizza eggplant with mushrooms	Gourmet Greek Chicken Salad
Saturday		
Breakfast	Bruschetta with Greek yogurt and tomatoes	Greek yogurt scrambled eggs
Lunch	Greek rice with black beans	Gourmet chicken with veggies
Dinner	Middle eastern cheese rolls	Aperitif with salmon and mix of vegetables
Sunday		
Breakfast	Tender frittata with herbs	Bruschetta with spinach, squash and egg
Lunch	Traditional tomato rice	Salmon with feta and veggies
Dinner	Super tasty cherry tomatoes salad	Stuffed zucchini slices with feta and tomato

Monday	Week 3	Week 4
Breakfast	Bowl with millet and strawberries	Bruschetta with spinach, squash and egg
Lunch	Greek rice with lemon	Beef stew with green beans
Dinner	Berry salad with burrata and arugula	Mediterranean panzanella salad
Tuesday		
Breakfast	Semifreddo with blueberries and dried fruit	Grain bowl with egg and avocado
Lunch	Middle Eastern lamb meatballs with onions	Nutritious halibut with veggies
Dinner	Spanish bruschetta with tomato	Mix of brussels sprouts and mushrooms
Wednesday		
Breakfast	Dandelion bruschetta and yogurt	Greek yogurt scrambled eggs
Lunch	Yummy rice with shrimps	Greek fish fillet
Dinner	Greek-style tuna salad	Salad with brussels sprouts and dried fruit
Thursday		
Breakfast	Tender frittata with herbs	Tender frittata with herbs
Lunch	Basmati rice with herbs	Lemon flavoured salmon
Dinner	Tomato salad with feta	Yummy cauliflower fritters with mint yogurt
Friday		
Breakfast	Grain bowl with egg and avocado	Dandelion bruschetta and yogurt
Lunch	Delicious pasta with cherry tomatoes	Baked fish with tomatoes and spices
Dinner	Mediterranean veggies salad	Tomato salad with burrata and prosciutto
Saturday		
Breakfast	Nutritious spinach crepes	Avocado Cheese Omelette
Lunch	Mediterranean rice with chicken powder	Greek chicken wings
Dinner	Nutritious salad with avocado	Tasty Greek skewers
Sunday		
Breakfast	Nectarine peach bruschetta	Grain bowl with egg and avocado
Lunch	Tasty sausages with peppers	Pasta with tomato and basil
Dinner	Delicious Greek pita with cheese and spinach	Asparagus salad with tomatoes

	Week 5	Week 6
Monday		
Breakfast	Nectarine peach bruschetta	Bowl with millet and strawberries
Lunch	Tomato macaroni with fresh ricotta	Gourmet chicken with veggies
Dinner	Salad with watermelon and feta	Feta croquettes with sesame and honey
Tuesday		
Breakfast	Toast with egg and avocado with oriental flavours	Nutritious spinach crepes
Lunch	Greek pasta with feta	Traditional tomato rice
Dinner	Greek fried eggplant sticks	Pizza eggplant with mushrooms
Wednesday		
Breakfast	Nutritious bowl with blueberries, dried fruits and granola	Bruschetta with feta cheese and watermelon radishes
Lunch	Vegetarian ravioli with artichokes	Greek rice with lemon
Dinner	Tomato salad with burrata and prosciutto	Tomato salad with feta
Thursday		
Breakfast	Dandelion bruschetta and yogurt	Bowl of oats with banana and chocolate
Lunch	Beef ribs in wine with potatoes	Greek chicken wings
Dinner	Mini bruschetta with figs and goat cheese	Mediterranean veggies salad
Friday		
Breakfast	Bowl with millet and strawberries	Greek yogurt scrambled eggs
Lunch	Italian fish soup	Traditional Chicken Parmesan pasta
Dinner	Berry salad with burrata and arugula	Yummy cauliflower fritters with mint yogurt
Saturday		
Breakfast	Nutritious spinach crepes	Bruschetta with spinach, squash and egg
Lunch	Beef stew with green beans	Pasta with tomato and basil
Dinner	Super tasty cherry tomatoes salad	Middle eastern cheese rolls
Sunday		
Breakfast	Bruschetta with feta cheese and watermelon radishes	Tender frittata with herbs
Lunch	Basmati rice with herbs	Fried rice with feta
Dinner	Fresh fruit salad	Tasty Greek skewers
Extra		
Breakfast	Nectarine peach bruschetta	Bowl with millet and strawberries
Lunch	Tomato macaroni with fresh ricotta	Gourmet chicken with veggies
Dinner	Salad with watermelon and feta	Feta croquettes with sesame and honey

Monday	Week 7	Week 8
Breakfast	Greek yogurt scrambled eggs	Avocado Cheese Omelette
Lunch	Salmon with feta and veggies	Greek style grouper
Dinner	Delicious Greek pita with cheese and spinach	Stuffed zucchini slices with feta and tomato
Tuesday		
Breakfast	Bruschetta with spinach, squash and egg	Semifreddo with blueberries and dried fruit
Lunch	Middle Eastern lamb meatballs with onions	Delicious pasta with cherry tomatoes
Dinner	Salad with brussels sprouts and dried fruit	Potato pancakes
Wednesday		
Breakfast	Tender frittata with herbs	Bruschetta with Greek yogurt and tomatoes
Lunch	Lemon flavoured salmon	Baked fish with tomatoes and spices
Dinner	Gourmet Greek Chicken Salad	Nutritious salad with avocado
Thursday		
Breakfast	Grain bowl with egg and avocado	Nectarine peach bruschetta
Lunch	Greek fish fillet	Yummy rice with shrimps
Dinner	Aperitif with salmon and mix of vegetables	Mediterranean panzanella salad
Friday		
Breakfast	Avocado Cheese Omelette	Toast with egg and avocado with oriental flavours
Lunch	Super tasty shrimps with bell peppers	Traditional Italian rice salad
Dinner	Asparagus salad with tomatoes	Mix of brussels sprouts and mushrooms
Saturday		
Breakfast	Semifreddo with blueberries and dried fruit	Nutritious bowl with blueberries, dried fruits and granola
Lunch	Vegetarian fettuccine with mushrooms	Salmon with balsamic glaze
Dinner	Greek-style tuna salad	Grilled Margherita Pizza
Sunday		
Breakfast	Bruschetta with Greek yogurt and tomatoes	Dandelion bruschetta and yogurt
Lunch	Rice salad with salmon	Chicken thighs with yogurt sauce
Dinner	Orange and pomegranate salad	Bruschetta with feta and salmon
Extra		
Breakfast	Greek yogurt scrambled eggs	Avocado Cheese Omelette
Lunch	Salmon with feta and veggies	Greek style grouper
Dinner	Delicious Greek pita with cheese and spinach	Stuffed zucchini slices with feta and tomato

Conclusion

So here we are at the end of this journey into the culinary tradition of the Mediterranean countries. What is surprising is that the Mediterranean diet is flexible and can be adapted to different dietary needs and preferences, making it a sustainable and enjoyable way of eating for many people.

It is not the classic diet in the classic sense of the term, it is not a question of following rigid rules to lose weight but of learning to eat, to have greater awareness of the foods we eat on a daily basis and it helps us to cultivate a new sustainability, therefore to eat fresh and seasonal food.

It is also a good opportunity to socialize more like in Mediterranean countries and to make our family appreciate this incredible cuisine. the Mediterranean diet is in fact a way of living and being. For these reasons, it is one of the oldest, longest lasting and most popular diets in the world.

In conclusion, thank you very much for reading and trying my recipes. I tested them over time in my kitchen and felt the need to share them with you. So, if you liked this manual, please leave me a review! It will help a lot my work, my future books. My dream would be to create a beautiful and large family online community with the aim of helping more and more people to achieve their well-being for life!

Thanks again!

Made in the USA
Coppell, TX
13 April 2023